A Football Odyssey 2:
For the Fans By the Fans

A Football Odyssey:
For the Fans
By the Fans

Edited by
Alex Alexandrou
and
Sean Fenelon

Kennedy & Boyd

Kennedy & Boyd
an imprint of
Zeticula
57 St Vincent Crescent
Glasgow
G3 8NQ
Scotland.

http://www.kennedyandboyd.co.uk
admin@kennedyandboyd.co.uk

First published in 2011
Compilation Copyright © Zeticula 2011

Front cover photographs:
Upper © North East Press Limited 2011
Lower © Paul Harris 2011

Introduction Copyright © Alex Alexandrou 2011;
Dunstable Town Copyright © Paul Harris 2011;
Brentford Copyright © Emma Parry 2011;
Montrose Copyright © Graham Douglas 2011;
Queens Park Rangers Copyright © Alf Mellström with Caj Hjelm 2011;
Hartlepool United Copyright © Denis Pickett 2011;
Perth Glory Copyright © Alex Alexandrou 2011;
Ipswich Town Copyright © Peter Simkins 2011;
Liverpool Copyright © Tony Wailey 2011;
Port Vale Copyright © John M. Bourne 2011;
Bath City Copyright © Gerry Dolan 2011;
Arsenal Copyright © Gary Sheffield 2011;
Sheffield United Copyright © Jack Simpson 2011;

ISBN 978-1-84921-114-7 *Paperback*

For Billy, Louie, Clare and Jane
and for football fans everywhere
who passionately love the beautiful game
and their clubs irrespective of personal hardship,
family pressures and the growing commercialisation of football.

This book is also dedicated to the memory of
Charlie Andrea, Photis Alexandrou and
John Lee, who all sadly passed away in 2010.

Acknowledgements

This second volume would not have been possible if it was not for the enthusiasm and support of a number of individuals and we are taking this opportunity to show our appreciation of their involvement.

Thanks to all the contributors to this book, who willingly sacrificed their free and family time to write their respective chapters and accepted the gentle harassment of the editors with good grace, humour and patience.

Special mention must go to Marc Griggs and Simon Howe who assisted Gerry Dolan with his Bath City chapter and to Paul Harris who has publicised not only this volume but the first at every given opportunity.

And thanks to our families who have yet again had to put up for losing us for many hours and days in the compilation of this volume.

We are indebted to all of you.

Alex Alexandrou
Sean Fenelon
July 2011

Contents

1

Fighting for the Heart and Soul of the Game – What is to be Done?

Alex Alexandrou and Sean Fenelon

In an age where the word apocryphal is frequently used, often misspelled and rarely understood it remains reasonable to suggest that certain games are generally held to mark turning points in the development of the game of football. The 6-3 defeat to Hungary in 1953 was meant to signal the end of England's supposed supremacy and (not so) splendid isolation. However, the single goal defeat to a United States team made of "foreigners" and amateurs at the previous (and England's first) World Cup was perhaps more indicative of the road ahead for our national side.

Similarly the furore following the 4-1 defeat to Germany in South Africa in 2010 may be less portentous than the 2-1 defeat to France at Wembley the following November. Bad enough that the vastly experienced Capello was seemingly outwitted by the novice Loew's somewhat basic tactic of drawing John Terry out to expose gaps in the supposedly solid English back line, but the spectacle of a France side that had been similarly exposed at the World Cup comprehensively outplaying a hapless home side suggests that, far from progressing, Capello's England are going backwards.

Add this to an increasing disdain amongst ordinary supporters of less fashionable clubs particularly from beyond the Premier League and a variation on the familiar club versus country debate begins to emerge. Traditionally supporters of clubs from the North and the West Midlands would form the bedrock of England backing. In the 1970s you could barely hear a southern accent on the terraces at Wembley but the England fan these days seems to come from a different breed of supporter altogether. Diehard supporters of clubs in the lower leagues feel little or no connection with the pampered playboy millionaires who represent their country and the simple fact that squads have been drawn almost wholly from a cadre of the elite clubs for the past decade is unlikely to ameliorate the situation. England has become increasingly like Italy in this sense and the advent of the Champions League with its concomitant spread of international club games has served to even exacerbate the gulf between fans of those same elite clubs from which the national squads are drawn. On the positive side at least the decline of international hooliganism (from England's perspective) has ensured that home matches are family friendly but this is a small crumb of comfort to those who once were happy to wear club and country badges in a literal and metaphorical sense.

Much of the responsibility for the reduction of interest amongst hardcore club supporters in the national side has to be laid at the door of the rapacious English media and in particular the red (and white) tops. Even the smallest of events is scrutinised to the finest degree and any distinction between professional and personal conduct is considered pretty much irrelevant with, for example, John Terry's bedroom behaviour thoroughly over-shadowing the (paucity of his) performances on the pitch in either shirt. Plainly this didn't happen in the (not so) good old days! In developing his seminal book about the Tottenham Hotspur side of the early 1970s, *The Glory Game*, Hunter Davies later stated in his *New Statesman* column that their players passed a naked girl from room to room in a hotel on an overnighter before an away game. He fails to mention the fact that this was only presumably between the rooms of those players who had neither wives nor girlfriends. Contrast this with the (allegedly) London clubs footballer "gangbang" and the Sunderland player party filmed on a spectator's mobile - where the former led to Max Clifford being hired as an agent for the violated 17 year old and the latter being unofficially released to worldwide internet acclaim - and a picture of the power of the 24/7 media circus begins to form. The plain fact is, though, the depth and (forgive us) penetration of the modern media in all its forms.

From the supporter's perspective, however, the inexorable rise of the internet can, in aggregate terms, surely only be seen in a positive light. From the early email threads of the '90s to modern message board phenomena the average (if there can be such a thing) fan has never had so much access to information and opportunity to vent (largely) his or (occasionally) her spleen. The world wide web contains all forms of human life and this is mirrored within and across the football fraternity. From individually owned and partially to fully sponsored blogs to proprietorial sites the breadth of detail on offer borders on the truly staggering.

Messageboards are legion and whilst they are almost directly responsible for the demise of the '80s Fanzine era their inherent ability to connect supporters of a single or in a limited number of cases different clubs can only be applauded. Whilst sites vary enormously in terms of both size and spread each will include variations on the following:

Luke Atme – whilst essentially everyone who posts on a social network of any description irrespective of whether they relate to football craves a level of attention, the Luke type is particularly needy often to the point where he will establish his own board or at the very least look to carve a niche for himself. This type will frequently overreact to the smallest issue and will sometimes seek confrontation as a means to generate attention and may have misbehaved as a child for similar reasons.

The Agent Provocateur or *Fisherman* thrives in the environment because most boards allow for anonymity. As a result this presents the opportunity for gentle (and occasionally malicious) gossip mongers and wind up merchants. Sometimes this can be highly amusing but equally frustrating for those who "don't get it". One wag was known to trawl the message boards of rivals only to deliberately confuse one of their favourite players with another similarly named (Steve Howard of Leicester confused with Brian Howard of Barnsley by way of example) with a view to seeing how many bites he could get and/or the level of indignation he could incite. Others will be purposefully racist or reactionary with the intention of drawing out the inner Nazis who are undoubtedly amongst us.

The Darth inVader, although by definition related to Luke above is inherently a glass half-full person who will generally dig himself into a rut of negativity to the point whereby when things are going well (i.e. the club is in a sound financial state or are winning regularly) he will be seen less often only to reappear when the rot sets in. Darth is often inclined to procrastination or does a boring job such as accountancy...

The Expert comes in two forms: the Googler and the Polymath. The former will know his way around the 'net and be a frequent visitor (and possible contributor) to Wikipedia whereas the latter will generally be older and have slightly autistic tendencies. Both will be amongst the first to participate in the frequent quizzes available on many sites and enjoy games of one-upmanship.

The Innocent Abroad is like the Jeff Daniels character in the film Something Wild in that he will wandering unwittingly into alien terrain to be either greeted with a virtual version of open arms, totally ignored or ritually humiliated. The smaller boards carry the greatest risk because they tend to harbour cliques. Often from the younger age groups the Innocent Abroad will tend towards a Darwinian outcome whereby he adapts or dies (in a virtual sense).

Statistics show that for every person making an active contribution to a board there will be upwards of five times as many just watching and listening, so safe to say Big (or little) Brother is out there. In one infamous instance members of the Sheffield Wednesday board sought to take legal action against a number of frequent posters on the Owlstalk messageboard.

On which note, at the time of writing, it is illuminating to see that Her Majesty's Revenue and Customs (HMRC) have finally received their due from the South Yorkshire club despite having had the right to wind them up previously. As with Portsmouth and Preston before them Wednesday have undoubtedly benefitted from the special status meted out to bigger clubs. Pity then that they didn't show similar patience when winding up Ilkeston Town for owing a mere fraction of your average Manchester City reserve's weekly wage.

Meanwhile the growth of unfettered commercialism continues apace with clubs seeking to exploit every metaphorical blade of grass available to them. It is difficult to comprehend now that until the 1980s even buying a club strip wasn't commonplace. These days you can barely move with a brand opportunity being thrust at you. Not only are shirts sponsored but so are corners! Even the traditionally pure Barcelona strip has sold out replacing Unicef with the dubious Qatar Foundation who presumably are looking to solve the ongoing mystery of stuffy noses.

Qatar itself is also taking centre stage on two fronts. Firstly as the controversial winning nation in the FIFA bidding process to stage the 2022 World Cup and, secondly, due to the related and perverse fact that the figure behind said win, Mohamed Bin Hammam, the head of Asian Soccer has been found guilty of bribery and corruption and given a lifetime ban by FIFA. The 2022 World Cup now appears under threat as a consequence.

As with the first volume, there is no rhyme or reason for this collection of essays. They have been written by a disparate group of football lovers who have an endearing passion for the game. The main difference from the first volume is that we have cast our net further afield and have included non-league as well as league clubs. There are two contributions from the non-league in the form of Dunstable Town plying its trade in the lowly reaches of the non-league pyramid in England in the Molten Spartan South Midlands Premier Division and Bath City which has reached the pinnacle of the English non-league structure playing in the Blue Square Bet Premier Football League. The stories of these two clubs vividly illustrate the precarious financial position non-league clubs often find themselves in but also highlight the selfless devotion and camaraderie that such clubs inspire amongst their loyal and some would say deranged and masochistic supporters.

There are a couple of vignette chapters that capture three matches in particular in Australia and Scotland in the form of games involving Perth Glory and Montrose respectively. They highlight the angst and frustration of a lowly Scottish league supporter and the joys of a holidaying pom basking in the raucous atmosphere of an Australian league game taken over by ex-patriot and holidaying Englishmen.

The reader will be treated to a continental take on English football in the form of a group of Swedish fellows who for several decades have had a love affair with Queens Park Rangers. Their take on English football and culture will make you smile and wince, often at the same time but exemplifies the enduring pull of the British game for those living beyond our shores. This is further encapsulated with the reminisces of an exiled Englishmen now residing in the sunnier climes of Western Australia with the journey taking the reader from the fortunes or misfortunes depending on your outlook on life of Hartlepool United in the 1950s to the poignancy of the World Cup Final in South Africa in 2010.

The adventures of Brentford and Port Vale fans bring out further dimensions of being a football supporter, notably as a female supporter involved in the politics of a club in relation to the former and with the latter not only having a life-long association with a club that is passed on through the generations but experiencing the emotion of the declaration of support in such a manner that it is life-affirming. As they say, it takes all sorts! The generational theme is continued in the Sheffield United chapter that shows how the mantle of supporting a club is passed on from father to son. The passage through childhood into adult life portrayed through supporting the Blades, with the son dealing not only with the angst of his father but also his own as certain games, particularly those involving relegation and promotion as well as vital cup games begin to shape his life and persona as a young man growing up in 21stcentury Britain.

The highs and lows of a small provincial league club punching above its weight are vividly portrayed in the Ipswich Town chapter. The reader is transported back in time to the glory days of the 1970s and 1980s when the club was under the stewardship of the late Sir Bobby Robson winning trophies playing an exciting brand of attacking football with a squad significantly made up of local talent and then back to the present with an acceptance that mediocre may be the best that the club can hope for in these money-obsessed times that football in Britain, notably England, finds itself in.

Finally to the Premier League and two contrasting chapters. The Liverpool story can best be described as surreal based against the backdrop of the city's maritime history and a love affair. It takes the reader through the great times of the club; the disaster of Hillsborough; its devastating knock-on effect on the club and the people of the city; through to the modern era and the disillusionment with foreign owners who lack credibility and have no sense or understanding of the history and achievements of the club. The Arsenal chapter takes the reader on a journey from the 1970s to the present day and how it has shaped one fan's life and affection for the club. Memories of attending matches in the seventies at Highbury juxtapose with work and family commitments restricting a passionate fan to only the occasional visit to the new corporate Emirates stadium and using all forms of modern media to get as close as any fan could wish to be to their beloved club.

We have enjoyed putting together the second volume of this particular odyssey and, as it says on the tin, it is for the fans by the fans.

2

Dunstable Town

Downright Dunstable

Paul Harris

'Downright Dunstable' is a phrase you will see referred to in 'Brewers Dictionary of Phrase and Fable', and as well as that their home ground is located off the Brewers Hill Road, and is named for Alderman Wally Creasey who instigated the move from the old Kingsway ground in the late 1960s. Downright Dunstable means 'plain speaking' and I am delighted to say that one of Trollope's most enduring characters is named Miss Dunstable. Well, it is easy to miss Dunstable's ground. When I moved there in 1988, the first job I allocated myself was to cycle to the town to order a gas stove and discover the stadium which has a memorable alumni in the likes of George Best, Kerry Dixon and Jeff Astle and a former manager, Barry Fry.

Yet with all this history, I found it was much easier to buy a gas stove as no-one seemed to know the location of their own senior team. As always a postman came to my aid and added a piece of information I already knew, that George Best, in the twilight of his illustrious career, played for the Blues in a 3-2 win over a Manchester United XI, in front of the still record crowd of 10,000.

Ironic though it was, the ground was located very close to my new home. My last non-league club was Haringey Borough, a club that came into existence after the merger of Edmonton FC and Wood Green Town, and famous for being the only football club to have a ground actually located along White Hart Lane, Tottenham. The league club is in the High Road.

The very day I moved to Dunstable, Arsenal, a club I watched regularly, being my then local team, had lost to Luton Town at Wembley in the League Cup. There was some local celebration, which was understandable as the Hatters were then Bedfordshire's only league club, but my private quest was to locate Dunstable Town. Creasey Park was by any standards modest, its stand having a floor of former railway sleepers, plucked from the still existing track bed which is now a cycle path. Its nether regions contained the dressing rooms and board room, all in Spartan simplicity and with the usual impecunious signs so common to non-league. What terracing there was equally modest. The seats in the stand originated from Wembley stadium and the later turnstiles had come from Maine Road, former home of Manchester City. They were notoriously stiff despite my subsequent attacks with WD40, when I was later assigned a job as turnstile man, I always reacted to the comments that they were virtually impossible to get through by saying that the machines had come from Maine Road and ' had not seen much use'. Totally inaccurate, of course, but it did raise a smile now and again.

The floodlights pylons swayed with a gentle sense of insecurity in the breeze, and the car park was bald of tarmac, having been placed over the spoil from the town's former gas works. The clubhouse was small, dingy but essentially homely to me; to others it looked like the set of Golden Gordon from 'Ripping Yarns'. Being a former Londoner and a regular at Highbury before all-seater days and exorbitant admission prices, I knew intuitively that I wanted to embrace the club of my new 'home' town.

An early match was taken in, a reserve game against Holmer Green as I recall, and the tea caravan did not bother to open. Behind one of the goals was a huge mound, spoil from the excavation to form the present pitch, huge by any comparison, and was later dubbed Chav Hill, since at any game, there would be a stingy group of non-paying spectators peering through the wire fence who whittled away their boredom by occasionally lobbing stones at the goalkeeper. Their sense of fairness or lack of loyalty saw them pelting the keeper of both sides. The few legitimate spectators saw a 3-1 win for the home side. But for me it was something of a conversion, I had become a non-leaguer, at present a spectator, but soon to be a supporter. Any dedicated non-leaguer knows the difference. A spectator pays his few pounds, buys his tea at the refreshment bar and then goes home to watch the news round-up of the professional teams. There is, of course nothing wrong with that. A supporter by my definition, is one who is aware that his local club, with a constrained budget, runs almost entirely on the efforts of volunteers and can pitch in with even a token effort of help.

Dunstable Town, like most teams at an equivalent or even a higher level seizes on whatever help it may receive, and so in time, I became thus involved. These were Southern league days and I became accustomed to seeing teams such as Weymouth and Newport (Isle of Wight) making the long trek to Creasey Park. The club though, had a long history of financial incertitude and it has survived two closures, one when another team Dunstable FC was pressed into action to fulfil the season's fixtures.

Barry Fry had a spell as manager and it was he who brought the legendary if wayward George Best to play a few games. There was also the emerging Kerry Dixon, still Chelsea's top goal scorer, who brought the club its record transfer fee when he departed to Reading for £25,000. He had scored 52 goals for Dunstable in one season and much later returned in a managerial capacity and still lives locally and may be seen at the occasional match.

That kind of stuff always finds its way into the programmes and we are glad of it, but the bread and butter stuff was the familiar struggle to keep the club going. You tend to forget the gobbets of history on a windy night when Great Wakering Rovers nick a 3-2 win after being battered all the game. What you do get and learn to cherish, is the getting to know all the regulars who turn up and moan at the team's ineptitude but come back the following week, or turn up at various away games, at clubs more well-heeled and with an anxious band of workers. I went as often as I could, sometimes guiltily cycling to London to see the Arsenal, but already I knew that it was Dunstable Town that was securing my loyalties.

There was a dreadful hiatus between 1993 and 1998 as when I arrived at the ground saw a 'closed' notice on the gates. Dunstable had bowed to the inevitable and had gone out of business. I may not be alone in thinking that the sight of an abandoned football stadium is a truly melancholy one. The stand was labelled 'danger, keep out' and having sat in it a number of times found that to be quite accurate a warning. Weeds grew tall, the sense of neglect was everywhere overpowering and for me it was a serious loss of a club that was relatively well known. I say relatively as much later when we were back in business, I remember a lady at Malvern Town telling me she had enjoyed a couple of oysters 'with me eyes closed' at Dunstable. She asked me if I enjoyed living at the seaside. It transpired that she had confused us with Whitstable Town.

So, we may have seen the light day in 1883, but news of our precarious existence did not enlighten everyone. It is really only since the 1950s that the Blues made a more serious mark, and a closure in the late seventies reflected the adversity a club will face with so many professional or semi-professional clubs within easy reach. Attendances were occasionally a respectable few hundred, but Barry Fry's first two games in charge pulled in below fifty on each occasion. There is a well known anecdote that Fry, receiving a ban from watching the team inveigled his way into a house close to the ground and watched the match from a bedroom window, with the aid of binoculars. Present Chairman Darren Croft and Paul Reeves were largely responsible for getting the phoenix to rise from the ashes, with Steve Kaye taking on the role of chairman. The club was briefly named Dunstable Town 98, an appellation now lost in history.

The ground was renovated to a certain extent but was still very much a poor relation to other non-league grounds in terms of infrastructure. But it was back, and so was I, forsaking my trips to Highbury. I did flirt with the original Enfield, but I knew that I was a Dunstable man, and it was only fitting that I should support my local team.

But rising from the ashes meant starting again at a much lower level and this was a truly memorable time for the club who marched through the leagues, winning a championship and creating a record unlikely to be bettered. The team went over fifty games unbeaten and that record was only ended in a narrow defeat at Tooting and Mitcham in the FA Vase.

By then my children were growing and were soon employed in helping me in my first supporting rather than more passive role as a spectator. On Sunday's we would go to the ground and fill bags with litter, with my shielding my offspring from the very visible leftover signs of nocturnal activity in the stand that had more to do with a passion not related to football. What officials there were about quietly acknowledged my small contribution and following this came one of the club's enduring myths – and I refer to the formation of The Regiment. The conception was not grandiose and it is really only a myth in relative terms. Huddling by the tea hut or gathering in the clubhouse, regular supporters gravitated towards one another, with mutual recognition. The consensus was that what was needed was an official supporters' club.

A website had been started by former player Martin Large and now expertly maintained by Daniel Crooke, and of course we all began to post our views and comments. Oddly we knew one another by our website 'handles'. Mine was Pipeman, reflecting my enduring habit of being a pipe-smoker. This followed a small family tradition, as my father had been groundsman at Marlow FC, where his only fee, for which he was eternally grateful, was a seat on the team coach to away matches.

When I was boy he had taken me to grounds such as Walthamstow Avenue, Edmonton, Leyton Orient, as well as the big clubs like Arsenal, Tottenham Hotspur and West Ham United. The trips to the big grounds were usually to see the professional team he favoured – Blackburn Rovers. The most enduring memory I have is a trip to Brisbane Road, where the Orient were in severe danger of joining Accrington Stanley in the wilderness. Some fans were walking around the cinder track with an open blanket, inviting the crowd to donate what they could. I remember my father putting his 'tobacco money' in the blanket, telling me that it would be a crime to let a club go down. I acted in like fashion, tossing in my pocket money. The next morning I found a two shilling piece under my pillow, put there by my football-loving father who spent that Sunday contemplating his empty pipe. I include this as it is a reminder that it is not just small clubs like Dunstable that feel the financial pinch.

The loyalty of my new group of friends is something I admire to this day, and we decided to form a supporters' club. We raised our pints and some of us included a toast 'To the Regiment – I wish I was there.' It stuck and it was considered superior to the other one, also culled from the television programme, 'Early Doors' – 'To our wives and sweethearts, may they never meet.' Thus the Regiment was born. The myth part is that our membership was extremely modest -embarrassingly so. But our present secretary, Scottie (his website name) soon employed his wife to make a number of flags and banners. We were not Dunstable Town supporters club, we were the Regiment. We even got hold of some replica shirts, in blue and white stripes, a strip we have reinstated, but I recall some people on the town glancing at my shirt and even asking if I was a supporter of Huddersfield Town or Brighton and Hove Albion. One of our successful youth teams had no confusion, as when they won a trophy, skipper Danny Ryan ordered his team mates to reverse their shirts for the presentation, as the kit bore the legend 'The Regiment' on the back and they wanted to acknowledge the funds donated to buy the kit following one of my sponsored cycle rides. Scottie had raised money on a sponsored walk to Hitchin Town and my next sponsored ride was to Chesham United on a tandem with a fellow supporter. We lost 8-1 that day and were labelled a pub team, a description they may have regretted when we won the return fixture.

This leads me to recall another sponsored ride I did to boost club funds to buy an ultra sound machine for the physiotherapist. I had a vague notion that such things were for use in submarines, but gathered names and pledges and set about a ride from Dunstable to Marlow. My elder brother had offered to accompany me and I readily agreed. 'Don't worry' I told him, 'when we get to the ground, I will make sure I get you in.' My patronising generosity was soon turned on its head. It was a bitterly cold winter's day and we looked forward to our arrival. Having accomplished the ride I looked for the gate man, who had been informed in advance of my odyssey. This gentleman looked through my greeting and instead approached my brother Christopher. 'Hello Chris, out for a run then? I didn't know you liked football. Come on in – oh and bring your mate with you.' As it happened the custodian of the coffers was a work mate of Christopher's and it did not stop there. We wheeled in our machines and I had explained to Christopher that I had chosen Marlow for my sponsored ride as our father had been a groundsman at this very club and used to cycle there as well. We secured the machines and, with a diminishing sense of importance, I offered to buy the beers in the clubhouse.

It was like a preordained script being acted out. Before I could speak the barman looked past me and was another to greet Christopher by name. Yes, another acquaintance, followed by an offer of a pint and 'does your mate want a drink as well?' I thought that if I shed my cycling jacket to reveal the insignia of my Dunstable Town track suit top it might lead me to some sort of recognition. Not a bit of it. 'I will have to leave you soon, Chris' I said, 'as I need to see the referee with the team sheet, along with their match secretary.' Christopher, who had until that point never been to a football ground in his life, except for a childhood visit to Tottenham Hotspur, told me to go and do what I had to do as he was busy catching up with another old work buddy. The officials were just completing their pre match cup of tea when I introduced myself. One of the assistant referees caught sight of my brother and the conversation took on a different focus when he hailed Christopher in the manner of greeting a long lost pal. Yes, someone Chris knew from High Wycombe.

It did not end there. Christopher placed himself on the terraces looking and feeling a little out of place. I stood with the Regiment, wondering if, in unison, they would call out in one voice, 'Hello, Chris.' They did not, but – and this is no fabrication, as when the ball was kicked out of play, Christopher left off from meditatively smoking his pipe to return the ball to a Marlow player. The player caught the ball and said 'Cheers, Chris.' He was another work mate. I was beginning to feel that if the Pope had turned up The Regiment and others would have asked who that old geezer was talking to Chris. My ego was thus deflated, which is no bad thing, and soon I was more concerned that we lost the game quite badly.

The Regiment were and are still a small gathering, but at least they were instrumental in many actions. They were the people who did the essential work around the ground on match days, and they were there home and away. I recall that in one season, 2002/3, there were three of us who for want of extra help performed the necessary tasks My job was to clean out the changing rooms, then to assume duty on the turnstile, sell programmes and write the reports for the forum and the local press. Scottie did sterling work on the pitch. On one occasion he rendered the ground playable by driving his car up and down with a roller attached to the rear bumper. Froggy, another Arsenal exile, who like me had decided to go local, used to line the pitch.

This work received the blessing of the committee, the manager and indeed the players. Our sole aim was never to see the club close again. There are some aspects of the club's previous financial history that are distinctly dubious, but a new chairman, Roger Dance was brought in and his financial input was significant We supporters had no money but we willingly gave time and work. Summers were spent painting decorating, seeding, etcetera, often with some players helping out, and of course we knew that this kind of activity went on in so many other clubs throughout the land, governed as they are by loyalty, pride and passion. We have a groundsman now, Will McLaughlan, who takes a fierce 'ownership' of the pitch and on more than one occasion I have seen him assisted by the chairman, vice chairman and various others. I remember when we were gathering for the coaches to travel to the Bryco Cup Final (a league cup), we had to wait for the then manager, Paul Reeves to finish mowing the pitch. Our star striker, Grant Carney, the present manager, was often involved in building projects around the ground, as was the current chairman.

My own contribution to the club becomes insignificant when I realise just what Darren Croft has done for what we call the infrastructure. He supervised the building of the John Sandford Memorial stand, a covered standing area in memory of a former reporter and supporter who died at a tragically early age and whose grave bears the crest of the club. Then there was the covered end behind one goal, and much of the concrete hard standing. This was erected with Darren Croft supervising and indeed it was a lasting improvement. One training session was to employ players to haul in endless loads on wheelbarrows containing a concrete mix – some twenty tons of it by the end. I may have painted the wall one summer but I take my hat off to those who built it.

Memories of the march through the Spartan South Midlands league are many, and I recall that when this team won the Bedfordshire Senior Cup at Bedford Town, we had so few supporters there that the team paraded the trophy in front of the county town's faithful. It might be appropriate here to mention that this trophy has been won the most times by Dunstable Town, even if there was an alarmingly barren period in this respect from 1896 and 1957!

Domestic trophies are always welcome, but the most senior league success came with being runners up in the old Southern League Division One, North. There is one trophy that did elude the club owing to circumstance. This was The Bryco Cup, the league club for the Ryman league. The team that had won two league titles in the South Midlands League had an astonishing run to the very final of this trophy, in 2003/4 beating, away, two strong clubs in the form of Grays Athletic and Sutton United, and the latter with a team patched up with reserves. I recall the two-legged semi-final against Hampton and Richmond Borough.

A decent attendance saw a narrow home win 2-1 and the Borough were fancied to make good the deficit at their own place. With the luxury of coach travel to Hampton, Blues supporters occupied a small section of the terracing and we sang 'Blue Moon' as the team triumphed 3-1 to reach the final, against Thurrock at Hornchurch FC. Why 'Blue Moon' we do not know and we did not all know the words, and it was a conscious borrowing of Manchester City's anthem. I said they would not mind as we had a couple of their old turnstiles. I do recall the victorious team, marshalled by Grant Carney, performing a Klinsmann type dive, which was mentioned in the Non-League Paper. The celebrations at the club house went on into the small hours. It was a grand feast for a team who played for only symbolic financial remuneration.

I also recall the chairman Steve Kaye constantly refilling my glass and I was ultimately gently led home by Scottie who told Claire, my partner, to leave me on the sofa. The players were euphoric as it was in a psychological sense a giant-killing act. I had asked our inebriated skipper if he had work in the morning and he said 'I don't care about tomorrow.' What was really gratifying was the notable sportsmanship of the Hampton fans who genuinely wished us well for the final and acknowledged defeat by the better team on the night. We yearned for the final and there was the awesome sight to the regulars of no fewer than three coaches booked and filled for our big day. If we ever had a coach before it held both team and the entire support.

Then, at Hornchurch, it rained and rained. The pitch was sodden and we feared a postponement. The officials were willing to give it a go, and many of us volunteered to help clear the pitch of water by whatever means. News percolated through that Thurrock, our opponents, with a reportedly weakened team embraced a replay date with more enthusiasm. There was a reasonable suggestion that the kick off was put back a few hours, but it was ultimately overturned. Unanimously, the Dunstable contingent were convinced that on the day they would have overcome the team that was to later turn professional. The date for the replay was put back to August and Thurrock trounced us 5-1 with a very strong team at Bishops Stortford FC. In many ways this is one of the biggest disappointments I have experienced.

Interestingly, there was a female official at this rearranged final and I do not suppose she was enamoured of one of our startled fans who said loudly, 'Crikey, the referee's a tart!' I will hasten to add that she was a first rate official in every respect. But when I look in our honours page of the programme and read Bryco Cup, Runners-up 2003-2004, I reflect that we were somewhat unkindly robbed. That Blues team was indeed on a roll and would, in my view have won on that rainy day at Hornchurch. But at least we had been promoted to the Ryman North Division One and there was some compensation when although we finished just fourth in that wonderful season, we gained promotion to the Southern League, Division One South and West.

Misfortune, of course does not always occur on the pitch, and there is one memory I have of bad luck coming in threes. A few of us went to an away game at Aveley, a team we had seen off easily at home. We were hammered 5-1 and as I sat in the clubhouse, our then secretary, Malcolm Aubrey, gave us the news that in the high winds at Bedfordshire, the roof of the covered end had blown off and a floodlight pylon had also collapsed. Not a good day I thought, but for the one and only time on my life I won a raffle – a bottle of wine and a box of chocolates. This, I thought would be a wonderful peace offering to the missus to excuse my late arrival at home, having surveyed the damage at Creasey Park. She was surprised and indeed mollified until my son told her it was a raffle prize. Collapse of virtuous party - and her chagrin made the bad luck indeed come in threes. There is always an uneasy relation with one's wife or partners, with pointed reminders that we would be better employed redecorating the home.

Anyone substantially involved in the work at a football club knows the demand on time and it has always been a difficult balancing act, but once it is in the blood we rail against anyone draining it away. Sometimes there occurs an incident that leaves one exasperated and one notable occasion saw us at home to a former Conference club. We were strenuously attempting to stave off relegation and a win on that day would help enormously. Scottie and Froggy were preparing the pitch and I was busy cleaning out the changing rooms. I normally had this finished well in time, but was called upon to line the pitch as Froggy had broken his leg and although at a hobbling stage, he could not guarantee straight lines. I did not add that the amount of lager he normally imbibed often gave away tell-tale wobbly lines. My effort was not outstanding but it was willing enough. I raced back to the away dressing room to mop the floors and was met with a degree of hostility from players of the former conference side, who had thumped us 5-0 at the ground they have since lost to a planned development.

I made fulsome apologies and explained my emergency pitch lining and was told it was simply not good enough. My rising anger was not helped when a player told me that it was bad enough to be forced to play at our 'awful' ground let alone change in a puddle or three. Normally, players and officials are full of understanding of the staffing difficulties and go out of their way to be supportive. I remember muttering something about them having to beat us before they can lord it with such misplaced superiority. I told him that he was a part-time player and like me he would have to go back to work on Monday. He made it known that given our first game 'at a proper ground' (and it was an impressive venue) they would have no difficulty in thrashing 'a glorified pub team.' Well, in Boys' Own Paper and in Melchester Rovers fashion, Dunstable won that match – in injury time. The flesh is weak however, and I confess that for the only time in my entire association with Dunstable Town, I entered the away dressing room and gave them the finger. The next time we entertained that particular club, still nomadic and in a league on par with us, their chairman apologised to me for the remarks made by some of his players. He even complimented me on the report I had written.

We had a fine battle with Bath City in the FA Trophy soon after and heartbreakingly we only managed a 2-2 draw, having gone ahead in injury time only to see Bath grab an equaliser in what we still say was Manchester United extra time allocation. We returned to Bath and had a shower, so to speak. The only team we could muster for the replay was composed of willing youth team players who relished the chance to play at Twerton Park, once a temporary home for Bristol Rovers. The Bath City programme editor had printed my report of the game against the former Conference club and we were treated with such cordiality and respect that deserves full mention here. They praised Dunstable Town, glossing over our limited resources and added that we were a team of some history who deserved to be where we were. Yes, I know we were thrashed 5-0 but I admired the lads who turned out for us. It was a mid-week game and I was not so proud that many of our then first team had succumbed to mysterious injuries or cited legitimate work reasons for their lack of availability.

This of course is not new. We supporters wear our crests near our hearts and we, perhaps unreasonably, expect the players to feel the same. Many espouse the club until an extra ten or twenty quid a week is waved their way and they are off to pat the badge of their new team. But I will never forget the hospitality shown by Bath City. Froggy, Scottie and I stood in the rain – perversely so as there was more than adequate cover. Our flags were out, with the unintentional joke 'The Regiment On Tour' I later went to one of the covered areas and I noticed that a number of amused home supporters took our photos and shook our hands. We had three visits to Bath that season, once to play Team Bath – and we lost the lot.

In fact that season in the Premier League we lost ten on the trot and we still went to every game, home and away. We had a chance to end this miserable run at Merthyr Tydfil's Pennydarren Park. I took my car with the ubiquitous Scottie and Froggy and the latter was asking me even as close to home as Aylesbury, 'We in Wales yet?'. That match is principally remembered for the heroic performance of Paul Taylor, our veteran goal keeper we called 'The Hammer'. This sobriquet is said to be endowed because of his hard hitting goal-kicks, but there is an apocryphal story that gives another version, which I will not relate. However, our lantern-jawed hero kept us in the game with a series of truly magnificent saves in an embarrassingly one-sided match, where our defending seemed to consist of lofting the ball into the sparsely filled stands. The Merthyr massive was behind Taylor's goal and they barracked him without let or hindrance throughout, especially when the ball was retrieved for a goal kick. We few from Dunstable were mesmerised by the Hammer's game of a lifetime and did not fail to notice that once the whistle ended this goal-less draw, the Welsh fans gave Taylor a standing ovation. Their chairman offered him a job afterwards, and he meant it. It is not the first time that our locally born custodian has been offered jobs with bigger clubs, but he succumbed just once. He played for Hitchin Town, ironically at Creasey Park against his former club.

Dunstable had earned their first point in eleven games, and the Regiment greeted it as if we had won the league. We did not tire of singing 'The Southern League is upside down', and we remained in the deserted terraces whooping it up like school-kids at the end of term (or teachers for that matter). We stayed chanting inanely until our secretary blew the froth off his beer, came out to the terraces and said 'Get into the bar you sad, sad, sods.' We barracked Taylor half-heartedly in that Hitchin game and he later told me that it was seeing Dunstable regulars – the Regiment - was a motivating factor of leaving the Hertfordshire club. He came home to us and has gone on to amass 500 appearances. So, there is, at times a laudable loyalty and a desire to play for the game and not the brown envelope.

The traditional colours of Dunstable have normally been some variation of blue and white, with a short period of all white. The current home strip is a nod to the past, with the blue and white stripes. The away kit was in disreputable condition but much loved – an unusual red and black hoops and became known as the Dennis the Menace kit. When it literally fell apart, it was replaced with the nearest we could get, a Milan style read and black stripes, and that too had an in-house name, owing to Froggy's indecipherable chanting. We were in the midst of a marvellous away win, and Froggy began to taunt the world with a chant whose lyrics seemed to repeat, 'It's just like shaggin' me nan.' There was a little relief when our inquiries, somewhat urgent and concerned, revealed that he had been singing 'It's just like watching Mil – an'. The pre-match lager or two has an adverse effect on his diction. That kit has given way to another, still in red and black, but there are those who still reminisce about the Dennis or the 'shaggin' me nan' strip.

With Creasey Park crumbling away, there was often talk of a redevelopment by the South Bedfordshire Council who leased the ground to the club. But it was clear from our visits to other clubs that we were indeed a poor relation. Vandalism was rife, the facilities were hopelessly inadequate, ground security merely symbolic. The close season saw Paul Reeves the manager acting as a foreman to allocate tasks to the volunteers. Being a schoolteacher I had the perceived notion that I was regarded as having little or no practical skills and what fell to me were jobs that were often bestowed upon offenders who were given community service.

Our groundsman was castigated by a probation officer for referring to them as 'the criminals', and he shrugged off the sociological lecture. The truth was that Will McLaughlan treated them with considerable kindness. There was one occasion when I was working alongside one particular fellow, who was emblazoned with tattoos and a fixed stare, and in his permitted breaks played the harmonica. We got on well and during one break I ventured to ask him what had been his crime. It was serious since he had been landed with a huge number of hours. He was an affable chap and a hard worker, and we often discussed literature as we worked. 'Well,' he said, dipping his brush in the paint pot. 'I came home one night early and found my wife in bed with another bloke.' He ended my pregnant pause by telling me he brained the adulterer with a saucepan. He then asked me what I was in for. I told him I was on the committee and was a little hurt that he thought I was a seasoned offender. But for the Regiment it was community service of a kind as uppermost in our minds was the sole aim to keep the club alive, unaware that ere-long we would be in a meeting with chairman Roger Dance who announced that the club had no option but to close for the third time as, not to put too fine a point on it, we had not even a pot to pee in.

We were crestfallen even though we knew that closure was a probability. Attendances were poor, with the exception of the derby games against Hitchin Town and Bedford Town, whom we beat home and away. As the gate man I had the habit of taking the receipts in my little cash box to Roger in the board room at half time. His brow was often furrowed and I know he would have liked to turn me upside down, and shake me vigorously, as if making more money magically appear. Roger was a local business man and had sunk a considerable amount into the club, and the much vaunted redevelopment were still fanciful drawings on architects' sheets.

The Regiment implored him to at least postpone thoughts of closure and to his credit he did so, since he knew that there was no club that made a realistic profit and often relied upon well-meaning sponsors, that have always been few in number. This may be attributed to apathy or economy but in part owes something to a dubious episode in the club's financial history which involved money laundering. The perpetrator later received a custodial term. However, against his better judgement Roger Dance soldiered on, and we were grateful.

Then the club suffered its first proper relegation from a league that involved us travelling relatively large distances and the coach bills were equally huge. Our only other 'relegation' at that time was being placed a league below as Dunstable FC were formed to conclude the fixtures of the newly defunct Town. Being placed in the South and Western division did not relieve matters since we travelled to places such as Tiverton Town, Cinderford Town, Stourport Swifts and a host of clubs like Sutton Coldfield Town, that were in the Birmingham area.

Pete Burgoyne and Gary Levy, soon to be the new chairman and vice-chairman later donated a mini-bus, but Roger Dance had often hired one and designated me as the driver. Our very own bus was decorated with our crest and website details and had a chequered career. I was forced to park it near my home as had it been left at the club it would have probably been on bricks by the morning. A kind neighbour allowed me to park it near his house telling me that it was quite in order as he was a Gloucester City fan, and thus demonstrated an empathy among non-leaguers.

We went to a tough evening match at Atherstone Town and lost after taking the lead. On the way home, the bus broke down on the M1 near Newport Pagnell. The then manager, Lee Cowley, swiftly organised a fleet of 'rescue' cars. The two female physiotherapists were gallantly placed in the first vehicle and so it went on until there was just Dean Falla, our youthful kit man, left behind. I was left like a skipper who goes down with the ship, but Dean was left presumably as he was not female and did not need any gallantry. The players, of course, took it all in their stride as if such things were bound to happen to our tottering club. We waited for hours for the low loader that I had great difficulty in securing. Dean, a sugar junkie, sucked sweets and I smoked my pipe. We arrived home at five in the morning and we gave Dean a bed on the living room floor. He went to bed in his tracksuit sucking a sherbert dib dab. He also told me that he was grateful that at least I did not leave him behind as I did once at Sutton Coldfield, albeit unintentionally. We sold the bus shortly after and the irony was that the man who bought it lives next door to me, so I see the bus every day, minus its once proud markings of the club.

Although I am consciously avoiding a potted club history, which can be seen in any away programme or on the internet, it is recent events that I am concentrating upon. Occasionally there is a collision with a more distant event, such as when we drew Staines Town away, in the FA Cup. This recalled a time when Dunstable Town made news on television football magazines. In an ugly game at Creasey Park, Dunstable were having a torrid time and had three players sent off. The manager decided to take the remaining players off and they sat sulkily in the dressing room, bemoaning what they considered a poor handling of the game by the officials. As a result the club was banished from the world's greatest knock-out competition for some five years.

It made good copy for my reports. I had by then become the club's official reporter and press liaison. The ugliness of that seventies match against Staines Town was repeated, which was a shame as I and others delighted in their fine stadium. Staines led from a goal that owed much to our veteran defender Bernie Covington discovering that his powers of recovery and athleticism were not what they were. Dunstable pressed hard and there was an incident where Mark Kefford was head-butted by an opponent and needed hospital treatment. The offender actually received a term of imprisonment for the assault, and the whole thing was recorded on video tape.

Another long term player, and a bit of a war-horse, Stuart Strange, bagged us an equaliser late in the game and it meant a replay at Creasey Park. Our Chairman requested that the player involved ought to be left out of the team for diplomatic reasons, but he was included in the squad. The Dunstable Chairman before the replay was making a token effort of using a vacuum cleaner in the board room, but he was not in a good mood, not least for his reduction to a menial chore. The inclusion of the player caused a robust exchange of views between him and his Staines counterpart and it seemed of little importance that the visitors won the match that lacked any kind of bitter confrontation So the ghost of that first encounter had not been fully laid to rest.

To play in the FA Cup is for players at any level a great privilege and provides great memories. We are at it long before the big boys make their illustrious appearance and of course all neutrals will cheer for the minnows. In 2004 we were drawn at home to AFC Wimbledon whose noble breakaway from what became MK Dons has received adequate coverage. Of course it was for us a huge game and thanks to the loyal followers of the South London team, we had our best attendance since the famous appearance of George Best in the win over his old club, Manchester United. Our capacity is put at 3500 and we were just a few hundred short of that number, photographing the crowd knowing it would be a long time before we would see the like again. We coped relatively well, aware of the difficulties nearby Leighton Town had when Aldershot were the visitors.

Often barracked as a team that has more flags than fans, we rose to the occasion and again there was footage shown on television. It was not entirely due to the football. We lost 3-0 but had the happy knowledge that the coffers were swelled. I was surprised and pleased that my Non-league Paper report was given a whole page and a half and the sub editor had given the headline 'Wimbledon On Winning Streak'. This alluded to the fact that a notorious local streaker who rejoices in the name of Moggsy, entered the field of play stark naked, hugged our goalie and did a slide tackle on the linesman on duty in front of our stand that has only been as full on a firework night Special when we hired out the ground. The scorch marks on the pitch were there for long time, but no matter. Moggsy got his few seconds of fame or notoriety on television and so did we, but by association. My first thought was that the club would receive a hefty fine for the slide tackle, with the charge of failing to control spectators. The assistant referee picked himself up with a smile and took the matter no further and has since returned to Creasey Park as an official and told me he took it all in good fun.

One point that rankled a little with me and the many people who had worked so hard that day, was an isolated comment made by a Wimbledon fan as she surveyed the near capacity crowd. 'Just look' she said, 'what we have done for this little club.' Everything is relative, I suppose. We later played AFC Wimbledon, in October 2006, at Kingstonian's now former ground, and we did well losing just 2-1 in front of about 1600 supporters. It was a worthwhile visit to a finely organised and ambitious club. I do not forget that they gave me a whole page in their programme in their feature on the visiting side.

Since I am involved with officials on a weekly basis I am at no pains to point out that, almost without exception they are dedicated and enthusiastic, considering the deprecatory remarks they receive on a routine basis. I was initially surprised to hear them commenting on the game whilst I sorted out their fees. I never regarded them as actually enjoying the match and of course I have regarded them with the usual subjectivity, but without them of course, we would have no game. It was a humanising factor to realise that officials drew enjoyment from their duties and I continue to regard them with the highest respect.

With the rapid turnover of players and even committee members, the club had to cast the net for a replacement to Roger Dance who took up a similar position at the former Aylesbury Vale, now just Aylesbury FC, and the most recent and deserved champions of the South Midlands Premier League.

In came Pete Burgoyne, head of a local scaffolding firm, a fact that stood us in good stead for another crop of infrastructure disasters. Paul Reeves and Darren Croft had been at the helm for some time and we also had as manager, Lee Cowley, now at county rivals Arslesey Town. Cowley had enjoyed great success as manager of the reserve team who won their league and went into the Suburban Premier League, which is of a good standard, with established teams like Basingstoke Town, AFC Wimbledon and Tonbridge Angels. Cowley moved up and the new reserve manager had a disastrous time in charge, often finding it hard to get a reasonable team together for the long distances involved. That reserve team played a league cup final against Salisbury City at Metropolitan Police FC, another splendid venue. They lost but with considerable honour and it was a bona fide reserve team we played that night as well.

Before Cowley's solitary season in command we appointed a young manager, Darren Feighery, who had proved his worth in charge of Hemel Hempstead Town's reserve team. He, as all managers do, brought in his own players, and in his case, a crop of untried players at this level, many who had played for Hemel's reserves. Feighery had a relatively successful time, and his squad were settled and enthusiastic. We played a pre-season at Alton Town and the young lad who was to be a star player for us, Chris Marsh, ran the whole length of the pitch after the game to thank the Dunstable supporters for their encouragement. One of Feighery's protégées, Dan Picknell, will always remember scoring a hat-trick in the FA Cup against Wingate and Finchley. There was a strong captain in the form of Stephen Pratt, and, indeed trophies were won, albeit domestic ones. The thrilling sight of these young lads winning their first league game away at the then Solihull Borough is one I savour. They also notched up a great win at the then league leaders, Bromsgrove Rovers. That season Dunstable were either in or on the fringes of the play-offs and it was a remarkable achievement, even if Hemel fans playfully referred to them as their reserves.

This success was not developed as much as we all hoped, as budget constraints, incessant player movement to and from other clubs all had its effect, but there were the usual memorable moments. For me it was the great honour of seeing my son as a mascot at Chasetown, a strong club, who enjoyed fame in their FA Cup games with Cardiff City. They took on Cardiff at home and we were playing Evesham United in a league match at Worcester City's ground after conceding that we would not make it to Wembley for at least another season. There was an announcer with a microphone who strolled around the terraces of this lovely old fashioned ground (it is so old-fashioned that I tend to recall it in black and white) and he kept us up to date with the score at Chasetown. Like all non-leaguers we let out a cheer when we heard that they had scored.

At Chasetown, their manager, an affable Charlie Blakemore, encouraged me to take a photo of my son lined up with the captains and officials. I was very proud and it was also my birthday. When Chasetown came to Dunstable, I went to greet their coach party, as is my normal habit and the first person off presented me with a large photo of the mascot moment which was a grand and appreciated gesture. Needless to say, it is a source of pride with Stephen, my son. We only played three league games at Chasetown, with two draws and a win. That win was one of the finest performances I have seen from a Dunstable team, and it was worth the prolonged barracking we received from a selection of youthful fans.

As an official of the club, I have had my share of awkward moments. One was on a long trip to Tiverton Town, who have a large following of Senior Citizens who were unfailingly good natured. We lost comprehensively in that game and a finger was pointed at one or two players for lack of effort. One was notorious for feeling no compunction to train but to view those hard at it through sunglasses. It was a bit silly as it was night time, and at the Tiverton match one of our supporters told him that he, the player, should walk home as he was of no use to the team in the game. The player was understandably very angry and, being nearest, I managed to calm things down a little. The supporter in question was being economical with the truth as he had not actually seen the game. He was rather taken with a fulsome wench serving behind the bar and became inebriated, since he had to buy a drink to receive her attention. Thus he stayed in the bar the entire game.

As we were leaving I shook the hand of the Tiverton Chairman and thanked him for his and the club's outstanding cordiality and welcome. All was well until the disgruntled fan, having failed to secure a phone number of the girl, told the Chairman that he, the official, was enamoured of sheep in a physical sense. Hasty apologies from me and a hustling of the fan onto our coach perhaps was the best thing to do. The need for diplomacy still obtains and being a little unsettled I was unable to appreciate the humour of our goalkeeper, the aforementioned Hammer, who grabbed hold of me from the rear, shunted a bit of simulation and said 'Pipeman, put this in your bloody report.' He tends to take defeats badly at times.

Then there was Froggy, who annoyed at the constant beating of a drum from a Chippenham fan, conspired to 'win' the drum at the conclusion of the match. I do not know how he did it, but it resided at our clubhouse for a while. We too have been the victims of 'trophies' as they are called. In a pub in Hednesford you may see a framed artefact labelled 'The Dunstable Trophy'. It was a lot of fuss over a nicked snooker cue. I have had a couple of pipes go missing as well, but I tend to have a careless streak when absorbed. At Felixstowe and Walton there was a win in the FA Cup and one supporter confessed on the coach that he had secured a trophy in the form of a plastic ashtray bearing the club's name. He waited for praise for his daring until about four others revealed the same conquest.

Hednesford were another great bunch. They had to beat us to ensure promotion to the a Conference league, and we had the audacity to lead for much of the game, which turned against us when Darren Sarll was sent off. We eventually did the gentlemanly thing by losing 2-1 and I for one shared the joy of their fans' pitch invasion to celebrate their success. The game attracted well over a thousand as well. I had been an official guest at the pre-match meal, as when they had come to Creasey Park, they were appreciative of the hospitality they had received. The basis of this was that at Dunstable we have the few to do all the chores and clubs like Hednesford have a legion of willing helpers. They were, by all accounts amused at my greeting their coach at our club, selling programmes and golden goal tickets in the clubhouse and later seeing them through the turnstile.

I always see off the coach parties with handshakes and best wishes, since it costs nothing and it is remembered positively. An example of this was in a poll on one club's website where, at the end of the season they ask their members which was the best or worst ground they had been to. I recall one fan who voted for us as the best in terms of received hospitality but the worst in terms that he thought on arrival that he was in a back street in Beirut. Often I have been saddened by individuals referring to Dumpstable, Duncestable or even the more obvious Unstable. I remember Scottie's car passing our minibus on the way to Clevedon, with his new home made flag stretched out in the rear window. He thought he was displaying 'Dunstable Town' but owing to movement along the journey it read 'unstable tow'.

Visiting other grounds is always a pleasure and I never weary of the relative opulence we encounter. At Nuneaton Town there were more stewards overseeing my parking of the minibus than we had forming the travelling support. With unforced humility I twisted my baseball cap in my hands as I was told 'Go into the director's lounge, you will see a table for your club, and help yourself to a glass of champagne.' We had a meal as well.

A good sized crowd, below their average, saw Dunstable lose 5-1, with the best goal coming from our Parys Okai's free kick. I made sure that I had a quiet word with their chairman and in apologetic terms advised him to expect a contrasting welcome. Our Chairman's is usually 'Go into our boardroom – that portacabin there - and I will put the kettle on once we have sorted the generator out.' The generator evolved from a winter disaster. Snow had fallen deep and crisp and uneven, and the sheer weight on our old flat-roofed clubhouse enticed it to collapse under the pressure. Our first reaction was not of horror but a curious gratitude. If it had collapsed during one of our vital hirings, there is no doubt that there would have been numerous fatalities as the roof was directly above the main dance area. Dunstable would have been national news for the worst of reasons.

But it was a sorry mess and that Beirut remark came to mind. The council, who owned the ground were initially indifferent, but repeated appeals from Chairman Pete Burgoyne eventually secured a temporary structure (which in a non-league sense means semi-permanent). We were given a cluster of portacabins which were designated for use as boardroom, (the original was damaged beyond repair), and changing rooms for officials and players.

Had Pete Burgoyne and vice chairman Gary Levy not completed a refurbishment of the smaller bar, that two would have suffered the same fate of the hire hall. This gesture from the council had a sting in the tail insofar as we had to concede the condemning of our grandstand. A world weary Burgoyne asked rhetorically about what else could go wrong. He was given an answer when within months, during high winds, a floodlight pylon collapsed overnight. It was indeed a crisis as there were still fixtures to complete before the close season. The council were called in and they promised to effect repairs, but a cursory inspection of the remaining pylons on one side were also condemned, Burgoyne solved the problem with the erection, at initially his own expense, some rather low slung lights placed on a Heath Robinson scaffolding arrangement. The enduring irony was that the portacabins and the new, temporary lights were seen as an actual improvement. No-one missed, except in a moment of misplaced nostalgia, the old changing rooms, with their recalcitrant showers of two settings, cold and freezing, and venomous lavatories that were known to spew mischievously the actions of the last occupant.

We also received some sympathetic coverage from the local press, who when we had won something, consigned us to a filler paragraph after five pages on the trials and tribulations of Luton Town. Visiting clubs were often sympathetic and comforted us with stories of their own leaks and jerry built facilities. These details were once illustrated by a mini-tour of Hertford Town, where they matched us leak for leak, so to speak, showing, if I may continue the metaphor, that we are all in the same boat.

When the housing development adjacent to our old railway line was under way, there was a sinister invasion of rats, their nests being disturbed by the demolition of the former automotive factory. The most alarming notice of their presence was when some determined members of the species came up through the floorboards of the burger bar and actually gnawed their way into the fridge, before making free with whatever it contained. I hasten to add that that little problem has been solved, but many of us remember the shrieks of Mrs Chairman when she discovered a dead one in the old board room. All this calls for some degree of stiff upper lip, a bit like that colour sergeant in the film 'Zulu' who tells a shell-shocked soldier, 'We're here because we're here lad. Do up your collar.' Well, those steadfast soldiers were a credit to their Regiment, and the Dunstable Regiment have done up their collars and faced adversity with remarkable endurance and it proved to be worthwhile.

The development was still a drawing, there were meetings that successive Chairmen had attended leaving exasperated and with no really positive news. I never wearied of informing visiting supporters and teams that 'when you come back next season, it will be a palace compared to this.' I began to believe my own propaganda even in the face of overwhelming evidence to the contrary. Those teams did not come back the following season, as owing to a serious infringement of a number of rules, including the fielding of an ineligible player, the club was given a debilitating fine and also deducted thirteen points. The team had doggedly achieved some good late results to place us just in the safety zone, but the deduction meant we were booted out of the Southern League to find ourselves back in the South Midlands Premier league, a division we had triumphantly taken leave of as champions some seasons before. When present Chairman Darren Croft had left us as manager we were actually in eighth position in the Southern Premier League, some two leagues higher in the pyramid. He is back now and the club is moving forward as every ending has a new beginning.

After the relegation Darren Feighery made a return to the club as manager and the club had no option but to make an assault on the South Midlands Premier to attempt an immediate return. It was a valiant effort, and we finished in a creditable seventh position, with the players expenses being defrayed by the club's bar that had been rejuvenated as a profitable darts emporium. Internal conflict led indirectly to Feighery's resignation, and he left to join Leverstock Green, a club not far from where he lives. Many of our players displayed their loyalty to him by following him to the Hertfordshire club. It was unfortunate in many respects as no sooner than he had left we had news that the development he yearned for was finally ratified by the council. The events are not related, of course, but the movement of playing staff and managers is just as rife in non-league as it is elsewhere.

But there was the thorny problem that once the diggers moved in we would have a building site and not a football ground, and more to the point we had no team. Even our illustrious youth teams had departed. One of them had emulated a previous squad who had won three trophies in a season. They had a talented manager in Lee Connelly who, with some reluctance decided to move on to pastures new.

As part of the development deal there was a ground share with AFC Dunstable, a relatively new club, who literally played down the road, or rather hill, at Lancot Park, known primarily as the headquarters of Dunstable Cricket Club. They played on an adjoining filed and needed a venue that had floodlights, even Heath Robinson ones. It is an amicable alliance and there is a distinct probability that in the fullness of time there may be a merger, I speculate here, but it seems logical to combine our resources, such as they are and be one club. We should drop the AFC and Town and be Dunstable Football Club, with the history intact. Well, I am no stranger to pipe dreams being an exponent of that increasingly rare form of savouring the weed.

But the here and now is a lot better than what it was. No team, the ground full of scaffolding, diggers and trucks, there have been great strides forward. Pete Burgoyne called a committee meeting and announced that he was passing over control of the club to new Chairman Darren Croft. Other personnel were drawn from the former South Midlands days and the new player manager was announced – Grant Carney, who was delighted to see his own son, Newman, selected for first team duty at Luton Town. Carney's reputation was secure. As club skipper in former days he was a fine example as a motivator and although he left us to play for a team in a higher league, he snatched at the chance to return to a club he has always genuinely loved. Being a star striker did not exclude him working strenuously in the past with Darren Croft on various ground improvements.

He assembled a squad and whittled the numbers down to those he considered will do the job for us. The League graciously allowed the club to play its first fixtures away from home in order to give the builders a fair chance of completing the job in hand But there was still a twist in the tail, when after just a couple of games as player manager, Carney had something of a crisis of confidence and requested that the club keep him as player and coach but install a manager of some experience.

After some consultation, a meeting was arranged with the two Darrens, Croft and Feighery and shortly afterwards it was quietly announced that the latter was once more manager of Dunstable Town, which was pleasing as Feighery had worked patiently and had awaited the overdue development of Creasey Park. It is a massive three million pound project, the money coming not from our impecunious number, but from the newly formed Central Bedfordshire Council, the Bedfordshire Football Association and Bloor Homes, who are erecting a large number of new houses adjacent to the ground.

For us it is vital that the ground remains Creasey Park and not The McDonalds Stadium or something similar. We want to honour councillor Wally Creasey whose vision enabled the club to move to the stadium that bears his name. Our own vision is to see Dunstable Town have a senior club that the town may be proud of. In my time at the club I have been underwhelmed by the lack of local support, but it is not something that causes that much surprise. There are those who occasionally squeeze through the turnstiles with a view that they are doing us an immense favour. Well, in a way they are, but at least we are still here, and despite two closures and a near as dammit third, we have been since 1883.

A town is often defined by its football club, and it is an integral part of the community. We want to see some palpable rivalry re-established with local rivals Barton Rovers, Leighton Town, the two Biggleswade clubs and Arlesey Town. Those clubs mentioned, with the exception of Leighton Town, have undergone major renovations and the result has been a real success. I am always touched at the huge pride they have in their resplendent homes, and my envy is of the best kind. Dunstable Town is emerging from the catalogue of misfortune and it is happening now. Ground hoppers, and they are many, will have to earmark us for a return visit in the future. Of course it owes a lot to the decision of the local council, who have plans to include a floodlit 3G training pitch, new stands, floodlights, a clubhouse, a car park and of course, new dressing rooms.

For me, all those years ago, Dunstable was a place I cycled to with the Cyclists' Touring Club, where we sat on the downs, eating sandwiches and thinking that God was in his heaven and all was right with the world. It was those trips that influenced my decision to move to Bedfordshire...and to downright Dunstable Town. In conclusion I pay homage to those in the Regiment as well as the small band of volunteers whose contribution is enormous but I am proud to be of their number.

3

Brentford

Memoirs of a Female Bee

Emma Parry

People are always a little surprised when they discover that I am a football fan. If being a female that follows their club and country home and away isn't strange enough for some people, then the fact that I also work in academia, where football fans are relatively rare, makes me even more of a novelty. The fact that I support Brentford rather than Chelsea or Manchester United is sometimes a step too far for some people. I have lost count of the times that I have had to explain that no, Brentford isn't in Essex (that's Brentwood) but in Greater London, and yes, they do have a football team thank you very much. At that point people invariably ask me the million dollar question …why?

So why do I support Brentford? It's a question that I have asked myself a few times over the last twenty years. I grew up with Brentford – my father is a life long Bees fan, although I can't remember him even going to watch them. I have often complained that he never took me to Griffin Park as a child – although I am guessing that taking your daughter to see a football match probably wasn't the done thing in the 1970s. As a young child I was dazzled by the likes of Ian Rush and even had a "Liverpool Supporters Only" sign on my bedroom door. My feelings at having a father that supported a team like Brentford was mainly ones of embarrassment, I am ashamed to say. In my late teens I lived near White Hart Lane and even bought a Tottenham shirt but never actually made it through the turnstiles. My football supporting was confined to occasional trips to Wembley to watch England play and, I am reluctant to admit, the odd 90 minutes from the comfort of my armchair. When I was about 18 years old, that all changed as one of my best friends moved to Ealing and started going to see Brentford himself. One Saturday I went along with him –

thinking it would be amusing to see my Dad's team play – and, as they say, the rest is history.

It's such a cliché to say that I was hooked after this one game, but that is pretty much the case. My timing was immaculate as this was towards the end of the 1991-92 season a few games before Brentford were to win the Third Division Championship. This still remains one of my all time favourite Brentford teams – I remember watching the likes of Dean Holdsworth, Neil Smilie, Gary Blissett, Terry Evans and Jamie Bates fighting for promotion as being full of excitement, but maybe that's just the intervening years blurring my memories. I can't remember much about that first game (in fact I can't even remember who we were playing) apart from being sucked completely by the atmosphere. Griffin Park was still mostly standing at that point and considerably louder than it seems to be nowadays. I remember the next home game more clearly, as I took my father with me. Used to watching less talented Brentford sides, my father arrived with very low expectations. At one point Dean Holdsworth received the ball, at which point my Dad said "oh come on you're not that good" only to see Holdsworth effortlessly turn the ball and slot it into the back of the net. My Dad's cry of "oh my God you are that good" still makes me chuckle to this day.

I should perhaps point out at this point, that I am not one of those football fans who can remember details of games that happened years ago. Most of the time you're lucky if I can remember who scored the week before, let alone provide pass by pass accounts of games from years ago. My memories of supporting Brentford are much more about the experience of being a supporter and my time with other fans than the technicalities of the game. Don't get me wrong, I love the game of football, the excitement of watching a player fly down the wing with the ball, a successful tackle and the sheer joy when the ball hits the back of the net (and yes, I could probably explain the offside rule if you pushed me). However, for me being a football fan is also about the people, about the camaraderie that you feel with other supporters about that "family" that I spend every weekend with for nine months of the year. As a supporter of a lower league club, it's also been about fighting for that club's survival; on a couple of occasions against individual Chairmen, but more commonly to overcome the financial burdens that most clubs experience at that level. More of that later.

My first ten years of being a Brentford fan involved going to occasional home games and even more occasional away games, usually Watford, Luton or Northampton as they are local to where I live. I went to all of these games with either my friend that lived in Ealing or my father, and rarely interacted with other supporters. It seems strange now that I did this for so long, but I think I just didn't know how to get talking to the other fans. The fact that I had now moved away from London and lived fifty miles away from Brentford didn't help. Around ten years ago this all changed – mainly because of a little invention called the Internet.

In 2001 I returned from a year's backpacking and out of sheer boredom started to spend a lot of time chatting on a Brentford message board called the "Griffin Park Grapevine". Within a couple of weeks I had managed to arrange a lift to the next away game (against Notts County) with a couple who lived near to me and was thrown into the social side of the game that had so far almost virtually completely eluded me. After a couple of hours of pre-match drinking I suddenly knew around ten times the number of Brentford fans than I had previously. Two weeks later, another away game against Tranmere and I was invited out after the game in Liverpool with some of the lads. This is the thing about football, especially when you follow a smaller club. People accept you just for supporting their team and once you get to know a few supporters you pretty soon know a lot more. It was at this point that my real Brentford "habit" began and I started to follow Brentford virtually every week, to every home and away game. That season I was one of fewer than 100 fans who made it to an LDV game away against Plymouth (my apologies go to the other passengers who shared that over night train home with us), and one of 84 fans that made it to a league away fixture at Blackpool (also mid-week). To this day, I have no idea how I or my bank balance survived. Nowadays, as work commitments have taken over somewhat, I make it to most home games and probably around half of the away games.

Being a Brentford fan is nothing if not a rollercoaster ride. Since watching us win promotion from the Third Division to the First Division (as this was the time that they reorganised the league), I have seen us relegated twice, promoted twice more and lose two play-off semi finals and two finals. It is still incredible to me that football can play with your emotions to the extent that it does. The experiences that stick in my mind are those that have involved celebration or tears (sometimes literally). I will tell of some of these now. Of course the games that I have chosen to talk about here are only the ones that particularly stick in my mind – Bees fans reading this will see these games differently and might wonder why I have missed others out. There are hundreds of memories of supporting Brentford that I could have included here, but I have chosen to select just a few. This is my personal snapshot of a few of the experiences that remain in my memory.

Any discussion of my experiences as a Bees fan would be incomplete without mention of the play-offs. Brentford have reached the play-offs four times during my tenure as a fan. In 1994-95 we came second in the league after Birmingham City but were cruelly consigned to the play-offs due to the fact that the leagues were being reduced in size that year. These play-offs produced both one of my favourite and least favourite memories of being a Brentford fan. I can remember beating Bristol City in the play-off semi-finals, dancing on the seats at Griffin Park and Ijah Anderson being mobbed as he walked into the New Inn, one of the local pubs, after the game. What followed was the final at Wembley against Crewe. I can remember painting my face with red and white stripes while sitting outside a pub in Harrow and then having to travel home with my red and white face after we lost 1-0. Brentford have never been successful in the play-offs. Since that loss to

Crewe we have lost another final, at the Millennium Stadium in Cardiff to Stoke and two semi-finals. I don't think there is a single Brentford fan who would relish the prospect of a play-off competition, despite the money that it would mean for our club. This is particularly ironic given that one of our ex-chairmen, Martin Lange, was partially responsible for the development of the system. I am sure he has regretted his support of the scheme on at least one occasion.

In 2003-04 we had one of the worse seasons that I have ever experienced, under the manager Wally Downes. A few weeks before the end of the season we were almost certain of the drop down to League Two. It is impossible to explain to a non-football fan how this feels. Every week you go to watch your team with the hope that their performance will improve and every week you leave after 90 minutes feeling depressed and despondent. The atmosphere in the ground changes completely for these games, away from the happy collegiate atmosphere to one that is characterised by shouting and abuse towards the players, manager and club. Of course, as paying customers, we are entitled to complain about poor performance on the pitch but I have never seen the value of shouting abuse at players during the 90 minutes of play. All this does is destroy the players' self-esteem further and if anything can make them play even more badly. In my opinion, booing and abuse should be saved for the final whistle. I once got into an argument with another fan as half way through a particular poor game he started shouting at the 16 year old substitute warming up in front of us "you're so bad you can't even get into this side". I told him to save him comments for the final whistle and was rewarded with a stream of abuse that I certainly will not repeat – still at least it was aimed at me rather than the poor teenager on the sidelines.

Going back to 2003-04, a few weeks before the end of the season, the Board finally decided to sack Wally Downes (much too late in most people's opinion) and replace him with Martin Allen. Almost instantly our form improved and Martin Allen became an almost instant hero – helped by his ability to engage with the fans through moves such as encouraging us to sing the Great Escape at every game and producing wrist bands inscribed with "PMA" for positive mental attitude. I can remember pulling into a service station on the way back from a draw away at Sheffield Wednesday at the same time as the team coach. I am embarrassed to admit that another female fan and I jumped onto the coach and threw our arms around Martin thanking him for turning our form around. Despite letting in a few last minute equalizers (including one at Hillsborough in fact), on the last day of the season we were left within three points of safety; something that seemed impossible a few weeks earlier. Thanks to a Thierry Henry-esque goal from Alex Rhodes we beat Bournemouth 1-0. We were safe! My enduring memories of that day are being in the club bar swigging champagne from the bottle and of my one and only participation in a pitch invasion. Realising that we were on the other side of the ground to the club bar and would never make to the bar before it was full if we waked around the ground, a friend and I decided to run directly across the pitch to ensure that we could make it in time. My mother had also come to the game that day and still speaks of her embarrassment when my friend and I leapt onto the pitch at the final whistle only to collide with another thousand fans doing the same thing in order to hug the players. We made it to the bar, even if it did take a little longer than planned.

A number of other special moments as a Bees fan have come as a result of games against bigger sides that we don't get to play very often. Most recently, our fourth round win against Sunderland in 2006. We have typically not been favoured with big draws in cup competitions but beating any premiership side is a memorable experience and thanks to two goals from DJ Campbell we progressed to the fifth round in that year's competition. This propelled Campbell to instant hero status, which was short-lived as his live-on TV performance led to his sale to Birmingham City the same week.

Another and much more recent high point in my Brentford supporting career came towards the end of the 2008-9 season at Darlington. While Brentford had been promoted twice before during the time that I had been following them, I had never made it to the actual games at which promotion was sealed. The 2008-2009 season, our first full season under Andy Scott, provided me with an opportunity to rectify this. Firstly, I should perhaps explain something about supporting a team like Brentford. As a Chelsea or Manchester United fan, after winning both league and cup competitions several times, you must begin to expect to win at least one trophy during the season. As a Brentford fan (or indeed a fan of most other lower division clubs) you do not expect to win anything at all. Brentford fans have this expression "same old Brentford" which generally refers to our consistent ability to mess things up. Therefore we don't start a season expecting to get promoted, although of course we hope and pray that we will be. After languishing in League Two for a couple of seasons and been in danger of relegation under Terry Butcher the season before, most of us did not have any great expectations of the 2008-9 season, especially given our limited playing budget. It was therefore nothing short of miraculous to find ourselves at the top of the table in April 2009, pushing for promotion. I can remember a few weeks before the Darlington game we played away at Bournemouth on my birthday. The sun was shining and we won with a confident performance. It was at this moment I think that most fans realised that we could actually win promotion that season. Of course Brentford didn't make this task particularly easy. On the Tuesday before the Darlington game, we played away at Dagenham and Redbridge. Knowing that we could win promotion at this game, large numbers of Bees fans had made journey – so many in fact that the Daggers stewards cordoned off an area of the home end for us on top of the usual away allocation. We virtually had more fans there than they did. I won't dwell on this game, but we lost in style, 3-1 and what should have been a promotion celebration turned into a mood equivalent to that at a funeral. When we went to Darlington the following Saturday therefore, it was with an atmosphere of nervousness and anxiety rather than celebration.

Could we really mess it up this late in the game? With Exeter and Wycombe breathing down our necks we couldn't get away with a performance like the one at Dagenham and Redbridge.

We needn't have worried. Brentford were 2-0 up by half-time after a convincing performance. The celebrations at half-time were like nothing I have ever seen – the bar was full of Bees fans jumping up and down and singing; beer flying everywhere. During the second half, I am not sure that any of us were actually watching the game. The news came through that Wycombe were losing meaning that we would be Champions if the scores remained the same. The away end erupted – just as Darlington scored a consolation goal. The home fans looked very confused that Brentford fans appeared to be cheering their goal! We were still celebrating as the final whistle blew – confirming that we were not only promoted but League Two champions. The players of course didn't realise that we were champions straight away but they soon got the message from the crowd. I have a photograph of the Brentford team standing on the pitch at Darlington with a flag that reads "League Two champions" – not that I will ever really need a reminder of that day. The long journey home involved several bottles of champagne and celebrations that will stay with me for a long time.

Most supporters will claim that their club has the best fans in the country. In truth, the fan base of all clubs is made up of a mixture of absolute diamonds and total idiots. Brentford has its fair share of both. One characteristic of fans of what you might describe as smaller clubs, especially those in the lower leagues, is that they all share a commitment and loyalty to their club. That is not to say that there are not premiership fans that are committed and loyal to their club, but I think the incidence of "glory supporters" is higher at the top levels. Generally, the Brentford fans that you see every week at Griffin Park have stuck with the club through thick and thin, through relegation and promotion, through near bankruptcy and takeovers by owners that may not have had the club's best interests at heart. I feel that this makes these fans special. That is not to say that I would count them all among my close friends. Over recent years I've noticed an increase in the number of younger, generally teenage, fans who are more interested in abusing the opposition fans than watching the game, a contingent that think it's ok to throw missiles at players or to pre-arrange "meetings" with fans of other clubs. I know from talking to friends who support other clubs that this is true of most clubs. Generally though, Brentford is truly a family club that does much for the community and has fans who support each other as well as the team.

A good, but sad, example of this would be the reaction to the sudden death of a popular Bees fan, and a friend of mine, Rob, a few years ago. Rob was larger than life character at Brentford, always to be heard if not seen at games – this earned him the appropriate nickname "Loud and Proud". The funeral was packed with Bees fans wanting to pay their respects, including several staff from the club and the manager, Andy Scott. How many premiership managers would turn up to the funeral of one of their fans? Supporters not only clubbed together for flowers, but to buy a flag that celebrates Rob's life – this can still be frequently seen at both home and away games – and to donate money to the British Heart Foundation in Rob's memory. It is this family atmosphere that makes clubs like Brentford special. We all know that Rob is still being Loud and Proud for Brentford somewhere.

The commitment of the fans to the club has meant that they have often pulled together in order to ensure the club's survival. Brentford fans have a long history of fighting to protect the future of their club, most notably to force the departure of Chairman David Webb in the late 1990s and to prevent a move to Woking in 2001. These campaigns were spearheaded by the Brentford Independent Association of Supporters (BIAS) which also led the creation of a supporters trust, Bees United, in 2001who have played a central role in the survival and direction of the Club since that time. A few years ago I made the mistake of criticising the role that BIAS was playing in supporting the fans' interests, and was basically told to do something about it. I joined the BIAS committee at the beginning of the 2004-05 season, heralding the beginning of a two-year period where my football supporting career focused as much on events off the pitch as they did on the pitch. At the time that I was on the committee, and later Chairman, of BIAS, the club was been run by Bees United, so our role was that of a "critical friend" and almost a "trade union" to promote supports' views and concerns. This meant that I, and the other members of the committee, spent a lot of time trying to reconcile the opinions of the Club, the Bees United Board and the supporters.

Let me give you an example. In February 2005 we were drawn against Southampton in the fifth round of the FA Cup. Needless to say, the demand for tickets was high and the allocation of 3,200 tickets proved to be completely inadequate to satisfy demand. The fact that the Club had failed to secure a larger number of tickets (despite the fact that more could have been made available), season ticket holders had not been given priority (as stipulated in the Club's customer charter) and that problems with the ticketing system meant that several fans who thought that they had secured tickets were later told that they had not, led to an uproar among supporters. It fell to BIAS to sort this out. Over the two weeks following this issue, myself and another member of the committee spent considerable time putting together a dossier of evidence about the ticket sales fiasco and took this to the Club. In fact, it took so much time that my colleague was in danger of losing his job at one point! In this case, it was too late to secure any more tickets, but the Club did issue an apology to fans and a revised customer charter, stipulating a strict order of priority for ticket sales was established. I am pleased to say that this has pretty much been adhered to ever since. Our reaction to the "Southampton ticketing fiasco" (as it became known) was seen as one of the successes of my time on the BIAS committee.

Generally however, playing a role in the "politics" of football can be a pretty thankless task. I don't think anyone who hasn't played such a role themselves ever appreciates the amount of time that people who sit on these committees spend working on football related issues, despite the fact that they all have their own jobs and personal lives to manage as well. In BIAS's case, at the time that I was on the committee, I don't think this work was appreciated by anyone. It wasn't a time when we were involved in any major fights for survival such as those against David Webb and the move to Woking and many people couldn't understand why a supporters' association was needed when the Club was being run by the supporters' trust. My feeling was that we were seen by the Club and by Bees United as a nuisance, by one half of the fans as trouble-makers and by the other half as not doing enough to fight against all of the minor injustices that were perceived to be taking place. It will never cease to amaze me how some people view you as to blame for their dissatisfaction with the Club. I will never forget how one particular fan used to "follow me" around one of the fan message boards and criticise every post that I made, whether it was about the Club or not. After two years, I decided that it was time to enjoy my Saturdays at football again and I stepped down from the committee. Despite people trying to persuade me otherwise, I haven't been involved in football politics since and have no intentions of doing so. I will leave that to people with more spare time and a much thicker skin than mine.

As I write this, it is the closed season and we are heading into our second season in League One, waiting for the fixtures to be decided and for the signing of new players to be announced. Our manager has suggested that we will aim for a play-off place this season, and as we were only a few places short of the play-offs last season so the general feeling among fans is one of hope and optimism. This is the beauty of football to me – the way that it starts again each August so that regardless of how badly a team has done in the previous season, the slate is wiped clean and the season starts with everyone in the same position. This season will also be our first season under a new owner as, while Bees United still have a major stake in the Club, Matthew Benham, a professional gambler and life-long Bees fan, is now in control. I am hopeful that this will allow us to be more ambitious in terms of the Club's future, but we will have to wait and see. Personally, I am getting ready to set off to South Africa for a month and follow England in the World Cup so my focus is very definitely on country rather than my club at the moment. However, come August, I will be back there at Griffin Park.

Thanks to Tony Cross for letting me use his memory for dates and scores – it's vastly superior to mine!

4

Montrose

A Tale of Two Games

Graham Douglas

5 May 1973 – Scottish Cup Final, Rangers 3 Celtic 2

It's 9.00am in the morning, High Street, Montrose and two buses are waiting to make the journey to Glasgow for the Scottish Cup Final. I hasten to add that these are not locals heading through to Hampden to watch their home team, Montrose, participate in the final. No, this is reality, not fantasy – one bus is full of red, white and blue clad Rangers Supporters and the other is a sea of green Celtic fans. And in the blue corner there is me, 18 years old, sitting in the bus with a group of friends, adrenalin flowing at what is hopefully going to be a great day out.

In total there are probably 100 fans leaving on the two buses. 100 fans who were all born in Montrose, some who have never even been to Glasgow, let alone Hampden but all expecting a 'Grand Day Out'. Come to think of it, I wonder how many of them had actually been to Links Park to see a Montrose game? Myself? I got along to Links Park on hundreds of occasions between the ages of 6 and 18 but there was something exciting and appealing at a young age of following a bigger team. I had relations who were born and lived in Govan and thus it seemed natural to follow Rangers despite the fact I was born in Montrose. And after all, I did go to as many Montrose games as I could but the 'passion' just was not there for me.

The game itself was won 3-2 by Rangers in a dramatic final and the atmosphere was unbelievable. The crowd was 122,714, the biggest I had ever been in and at the age of 18, I was in heaven. In football terms, things could not have been better. At that time I was sure that no feeling could surpass my excitement as Tam Forsyth scored the winner.

For the record, that season Montrose reached the Quarter Final, losing 4-1 at home to Dundee in front of a record crowd of 8,983.

16 January 2010 - Scottish Division 3, Montrose 4 Stranraer 5

Fast forward from 1973 to 2010. It's a cold, blustery day at Links Park Montrose for the Scottish League Division Three fixture against Stranraer. The crowd is a paltry 250, probably due to the fact that Mo have hardly encouraged locals to attend with a home record which reads played 9, won 0, drawn 3, lost 6. Maybe, just maybe this will be the day that Mo finally get their first home win of the season? Maybe this will be the day that when I go back to work on the Monday in Edinburgh, I will not be ridiculed? Maybe all the expense of travel from Edinburgh to home games will be worthwhile? Maybe Jeff Stelling on Sky Sports will not be able to poke fun of our run of losses?

As Stranraer take a 2-0 lead after only seven minutes, I think back to the Scottish Cup Final of 1973, ' The Glory Hunting' as non Old Firm fans call it, of the huge crowd, atmosphere, large stadium, even some silky skills on the pitch. I wonder why I gave it all up to go back to supporting my local team? After all, I am standing behind the goal at Links Park, cold and miserable as my team is producing yet another abysmal performance. The punters around me scream for the head of manager Steven Tweed and question if some of the players could cut it in a pub league let alone Division 3. I am ready to leave and never return; I am going back to watch 'the big boys'...

...and then, suddenly, Maitland and Campbell score for Montrose and all is rosy again. The half time pie and tea suddenly taste excellent as I anticipate an even greater comeback after the break. In the second half Tosh scores from the penalty spot in sixty-seven minutes then completes his double in seventy minutes. There is a rush down the terracing from the small band of Mo fans behind the goal. Celebrating that winner in the 1973 Scottish Cup Final? Forget it! Nothing compares to this moment I have been waiting for all season to celebrate. The start of the climb off the bottom of the league, the dawning of a new era, the end of being the butt of jokes...

...except somebody forgot to tell the Stranraer players. Two goals ahead with twenty minutes to go, tick tock, fifteen minutes left to hold out. In seventy-five minutes, Stranraer pull one back to make it 4-3. Ten minutes to go and surely Mo will hold on to the lead? But no, with five minutes left, Stranraer score again and all the Mo fans know what to expect. The wild celebrations in the covered end behind the goal are replaced by a nervous silence. We know what is going to happen and it does.

Romauld Bouadji, now there is a grand name especially for a Division 3 player. Romauld Bouadji, how could you? Eighty-nine minutes and the ball screams into the Mo net. Talk about a sinking feeling…words cannot describe it. It all seems to happen in slow motion, a bad dream, worse than listening to a Britney Spears CD, worse than eating an Edinburgh white pudding, worse than winning a weekend break at Arbroath. The home support troop out dejected. I am devastated – how can one late winner cause so much pain?

But you know what, an hour later the result makes me even more determined to support Montrose and if we lose the following week, bring it on. There is something perverse about watching a losing team week after week. It reminds me of the 9-0 defeat to Hibs in the League Cup at Easter Road a few years ago when, with a few minutes to go, the Montrose fans sang 'We want ten!'

So to get back to the point I am really trying to make…it's ok to support whoever you want, even if it is because you like their strip. And who is your local team? Should those born in Linlithgow support The Rose or trek to Tynecastle to watch Hearts? The number of fans on buses which leave Montrose for Aberdeen, Rangers, Celtic and Dundee United games could add 100 to the crowds at Links Park. That's fine but I would urge as many as possible to at least go to support the smaller teams when it is possible. If you are not going to see your designated 'big team' any Saturday, pop along to Links Park and feel a part of your local community.

Each season, I travel a few times down to Premiership games to experience different stadiums and it is brilliant but you know what, I get just as much satisfaction at the away Montrose games I can get to. It is great to be one of a small group – I counted ten away supporters at an Annan – Montrose game in season 2008/09. Better even than the 122,000 crowd at Hampden all these years ago-' Mon the Mo.

For the record - and it pains me to write this - the results of the first 14 Montrose home games of Season 09/10 were as follows:

Elgin	1-1
Forfar	0-2
Albion	0-0
East Stirling	0-3
Queens Park	1-2
Livingston	0-3
Stranraer	1-1
Berwick	1-3
Annan	0-0
Stranraer	4-5
East Stirling	0-1
Queens Park	1-2
Elgin	0-4
Albion	0-0

5

Queens Park Rangers
This Is Not About The Silly Season – Just A Story About Crazy Weekends

Alf Mellström with Caj Hjelm

Guys, this is my last football trip to London. It's the 20th time and, although it is always a lot of fun, it is time to break the tradition and do something else. We can go to other places to watch football, why not Barcelona or Milano?

It is early November 2007 and Caj Hjelm has spoken. Everyone in the group realises that there will be hardly any trips without Caj, who has been keeping it all together, before and after the trips. He alone has been organising all the practical details. But Caj is unquestionably the group leader and everyone respects his decision.

When the Winter of 2007/2008 has passed some of the guys want to speak to Caj. There has been a lot of thinking going on, and some of the guys are not comfortable with the idea of giving up London as our annual venue for football. Now the new found arguments for it are put to the test, and it went something like this:

We've been to London every Autumn for the past 15 years. We still haven't learned our way round the city, and we certainly have not yet mastered the language. So what's the point of going to new places where we certainly won't find our way around or learn the language?

Since then, we have returned to London in 2008 and 2009, and 2010 is a given!

In order to describe how the interest in English football became so huge in Sweden, we will take you back to 1969. This is when Swedish television began broadcasting a live football match every Saturday from the top English division in the form of the now legendary programme *Tipsextra*. This was of course before the many choices we are faced with today on the myriad of commercial channels, and the interest in English football grew rapidly. At this time, football was mainly a male interest and *Tipsextra* certainly caused tension amongst Swedish families. For many Swedish men, *Tipsextra* was a must, and the programme was usually accompanied by a few pints in front of the telly. The enthusiasm for *Tipsextra* amongst Swedish women was somewhat more constrained!

So what's the relation between QPR and a small Swedish town? In the autumn of 1977, Caj, then manager of Swedish football club Nyköpings BIS, went to research locations for a training camp. The travel agent had good contact with the captain of QPR, John Hollins, which gave Caj the opportunity to be present at training and a game at the London club. That game saw QPR beat Liverpool 2-0 at a crowded Loftus Road and from that point onwards, Caj became a huge fan of the club.

A special memory for Caj, who at the time was a young, ambitious and newly educated trainer, was Stan Bowles' warm up. During his training, Caj had been taught the importance and seriousness of a good warm up. Stan Bowles did not really live up to it in the time leading up to the start of the match against Liverpool. Stan Bowles obviously did not attend the same school as Caj, but calmly sauntered towards the centre of the pitch, where he stood with his arms crossed in front of the photographers. That was it! That was the warm up. Stan Bowles played a magnificent game and scored one of the goals against Liverpool.

The contact with John Hollins at QPR continued, which meant that Caj got to visit the club both in 1978 and 1979. During a whole autumn week, Caj studied QPR in training and matches The next phase of this contact came when the Swedish Football Association arranged an educational week for elite Swedish managers in December 1979. Speakers at this event were, amongst others, Terry Venables and Alan Harris. At that time they were both working in building up Crystal Palace, an investment largely based around the club developing its own young players. After Terry Venables and Alan Harris took over QPR in 1980, Caj's relationship with them deepened and he got the opportunity to follow QPR in smaller, continuous spells each year during a five-year period.

Another big memory for Caj is that he received a scholarship which meant he could study Terry Venables' and Alan Harris' work at Barcelona. It was the first time Englishmen were responsible for a major Southern European club and Caj's project was to write an essay on how an English coach succeeded at a top club in Southern Europe.

Over the next couple of decades, Caj continued to visit QPR one week every autumn, and got to know a lot of managers and staff, such as Jim Smith, who went by the nickname, *The Bald Eagle*, Trevor Francis, Don Howe, Gerry Francis and Ian Dowie. All well known names on the English football circuit that Caj has had the opportunity to get to know.

Caj's most memorable game is definitely from 1982. QPR managed to get to the final of the FA Cup and he got to see QPR draw 1-1 against Tottenham at Wembley. QPR lost the replay, but Caj did not have to experience that live as he had returned home to Sweden by then. Another event from 1982 that sticks in Caj's memory is that of QPR, being the first big club in England to lay down an artificial grass pitch at Loftus Road, something that did not amuse visiting teams.

Caj has of course transferred his love for QPR to his family For his son Niklas' 30th birthday, he brought Niklas to London to study QPR during a week in the same way as Caj had done near 30 years earlier. Today, Niklas is the head coach of Nyköpings BIS.

So how did our trips throughout the years begin? Well, in 1987, Caj was responsible for football in Nyköpings BIS while also managing the club's junior team (17-18 years). It was then decided that the junior team and all the staff would finish off the season with a trip to London. The journey started by bus from Nyköping to Gothenburg (400 km) followed by a 24 hour ferry journey that took us over to Harwich. After this, there were two days in London, and then the journey home again.

It was the travel agency that decided the game we got to watch, and during the years we have managed to see most of London's teams in action. But outwith this, Caj always made sure we got to see QPR play or practice. He made sure everyone felt obliged to experience QPR! Through this mild enforcement, many team leaders from Nyköpings BIS have now got a good relationship with the West London club.

Going to London with about 30 boys aged 17-18 could be described as a bit of a risk. But everyone has managed this very well throughout the years. Sure, there have been a few moments. One was when Caj, late at night, was called into the hotel manager's office. The reason for this was that some of our boys were being too noisy in a hotel corridor. When Caj went to investigate what was going on, he saw that there were a few over-ambitious team players, who through their own initiative, were practicing short distance speed, stop and start runs, in the hotel corridor where they had placed traffic cones. Ambitious, but perhaps ill-suited late night activity. The hotel manager's understanding that young boys take every opportunity to develop their footballing skills was, however, limited.

The last trip with a junior team took place in the year 2000. It was a dignified finale in every way. We managed to win over a combined second/youth team from QPR where the legend Ian Dowie played at the time.

Staff members who went to London with the junior teams throughout the years, appreciated the trips as much as the players. For us, it was hard not to look forward to a weekend in London at the beginning of November so we decided to keep this fine tradition going amongst the older generation. So, every autumn since the year 2000, London's been visited by a particular group of gentlemen who have a shared sense of passion for two things – football and beer.

Who are we? The group upholding this fine tradition is filled with people who have or have had staff duties with the Nyköpings BIS club. You could say that the "hard core" consists of:

Caj Hjelm (Cajan), who of course has already presented to the reader. He is the obvious trip leader and the force that keeps it all together. For many years, Caj has been one of Nyköpings BIS leading members. For a number of years, through different periods, he has been the manager of our first team. He has also been head of youth development at the club. Today he manages the ladies first team.

Bertil Nilsson (Belle) is the group's elder statesman, a really nice man who always has a smile on his face and make's sure the group is in good spirits. Belle is pretty decent at bowling, something which he has never managed to prove in the Queensway bowling alley. This is probably the only time when his good spirit is put to the test. Belle is still a much appreciated first team staff member.

Curt Hjelm (Curre) is the younger, but in no way smaller brother of Caj. Curre is a large man with a big heart that beats for Nyköpings BIS. He also has an incredibly strong voice, which is sometimes good, sometimes not so. In fact, Curre has been sent off due to his voice being perceived as aggressive when nothing could be further from the truth. It's just that Curre's voice would still be booming when whispering. Curre too, is still active within Nyköpings BIS.

Kjell Johansson (Dutta) is the ultimate organiser, with everything in order that needs to be in order for a functioning football team. Having worked as an electrician for many years, I think it is safe to say that Dutta is definitely better at complicated electric installations than speaking English. We'll get back to this.

Jan-Åke Andersson (Nocke) is the financial genius of the group, who has had some good trades on the stock market. Nocke is not the loudest by any means, but he often has a clever and funny comment to spare. For all our trips, Nocke has been the inseparable room mate of Dutta. Nocke has been part of the staff at both junior and first team level, but is no longer active at the club.

My name is Alf Mellström (Affe). I am the one with the least staff member experience in the group. For some years, I was part of the staff around the junior side and I have been a board member at the club. However, my work has limited my level of activity, and I have not been active at the club for quite some time. But I have never been able to let go of our trips to London, and cherish every time we meet up. Despite not seeing everyone on a regular basis, it always feels the same when we gather to go to London.

There have been a few others who have come along for the ride but not on a regular basis. We are usually about ten guys. The Chairman of Nyköpings BIS, Lars Elmsäter (Elmis), has also made the trip but not every year. Elmis is perhaps besides Caj, the one person who has meant the most to Nyköpings BIS. He has now been the Chairman for a few years, but before this he was a successful player and first team manager at the club.

The London trip is the reward for those active within the club. Anyone with the insight of the amount of work it takes on all levels to run a smaller football club, also realises that the level of financial rewards are slim or non-existent. This is a way for the club to show appreciation to those who put the hours in to maintain it. Those not active, obviously pay for the trip themselves.

The group is genuinely male, anything else is unthinkable. At one point, a friend of ours was in London with his family and we agreed that he should join our traditional pub crawl. We set a time and a place to met our mutual friend. However, he did not turn up alone, but had his wife and daughter with him. A serious crime of etiquette according to the unwritten laws of this group. We were terribly upset, but being basically polite people, we never once addressed our friend's mistake. However, we have on many occasions discussed this issue, and we expect something like this will never happen again. We also hope that the wife and daughter of our friend were not traumatised by the event.

We have thought a lot about the much discussed airline Ryanair's decision to set up at Skavsta airport, approximately 10km outside Nyköping. To some extent, I am sure it has to do with the proximity of Stockholm, but we are also in agreement that it could have something to do with our fine tradition of our annual trip to London to watch football and enjoy ourselves that is part of the Ryanair's decision. But we are not sure how much Michael Leary is aware of our trips.

We've seen a lot of football throughout the years in London and its surrounding areas. Apart from all the QPR games, we have seen all the London teams in action at their respective grounds apart from Charlton. For some reason, there's never been an opportunity to visit The Valley, but we hope to get there soon. And we have almost seen Millwall play at their new stadium. Almost means that me and Caj went on a pretty steep journey on the London subway system to get to The New Den, where they were to play Nottingham Forrest. We looked forward with great anticipation to the experience, The New Den and its accompanying fans. When trying to buy tickets we were kindly but strongly informed that this was not possible unless we could show membership of either Millwall's or Nottingham Forest's official supporters club. We could not, and the staff could not let us in to the stadium. The actual game was considered "high risk" with only official supporters club members able to watch the game.

So, being considered a "high risk" and somewhat subdued, we planned the afternoon over a pint. It didn't take long. We decided to go to White Hart Lane where Spurs were playing. Some of our mates had tickets for that game and were already there. We had no tickets and knew that we were pressed for time to make it for kick-off. But just fifteen minutes after kick-off we sat down inside White Hart Lane. There was no problems in getting tickets since the game had already started and the price of tickets on the black market was decent.

Throughout our years of watching football in London we have witnessed big developments. One very obvious one is the stadiums and the pitches. In the early nineties the pitches were usually in a really poor condition and the terraces were ill-prepared. Today, the stadiums are newly built and the pitches are almost always near perfect.

Forgive us, British citizens, but the influx of players from other countries has a had a tremendously positive impact on the game in the UK. In the early years of our annual pilgrimage, it was really quite rare and exclusive to watch players from other European countries, never mind players from South America and Africa. Today the Premier League and The Championship are globalised and this has, according to us, been an immensely positive football development.

We also believe the hiring of international managers and coaching staff has been positive. The early British strategy of long balls up the field from defenders or goalkeeper, received out on the wing, followed by a cross and scramble felt stereotypical and not so entertaining.

The Premier League, along with La Liga, are without doubt the best football leagues in the world. Since the early nineties we have seen huge developments in technique and game intelligence, while the quintessential nature of British football has been maintained, that is high intensity, tempo and an impressive fighting spirit. This makes British football great for watching and that is the reason why us Swedes and many others continue to love British football.

A less positive development in all of this is of course the ticket prices and the limited accessibility of tickets. Plainly speaking, football in the UK has became bloody expensive. Of course we deal with the high prices, as we only come to watch football once a year, but how is it possible for people with families and several interested family members to afford to see football live in England? Our conclusion is that it must be impossible without a seriously good income. Our theories may be disputed by the consistently filled stadiums around England, but we also believe it is shift in clientele. But football in England has definitely developed into a commercial entertainment industry and we question how it will continue like this.

Traditions are important to keep. Our trips are not about innovations and developments. No, comfort and recognition is more our game. As such, the whole crew will have to start the day off at Skavsta airport with a Jägermeister and hot dog at 05.30 in the morning. There is no point in questioning whether it tastes good or not, it is simply a tradition every year. Another tradition is that on the Friday night we visit certain pubs around Bayswater. The last pub we visit is The Swan on Bayswater Road. For many years, the slightly overweight

George was the main attraction. He had a remarkable ability to make happy, slightly drunk people from all over the world sing songs from their own country, accompanied by George on the piano. George created a great spirit and he had an amazing repertoire. I think the idea was to experience a genuine English pub. That wasn't really the case though. We met a lot of people here, but rarely someone from the UK. Still, we played our part and had a great time during late Friday evenings at The Swan. A few years ago, we were informed that George had died in a traffic accident. Very sad news, but we were not surprised of his passing, although we were convinced he would suffer a heart attack, weighing in at almost 200 kilos. But we remember him with joy. We have visited The Swan after his passing, but it is not the same anymore.

Another tradition is that every year we have contract negotiations with staff members. At the start of the trip, most members are pretty sure that they will not take an active part in the club anymore. The negotiations usually take place on the Sunday morning in Hyde Park, starting at Bayswater Road. When the group gets to the other side of the park, the negotiations are concluded in front of the statue of Prince Albert on the south side of Hyde Park. The negotiations almost always end up with everyone continuing one more year, under the same terms and conditions as last year, including a weekend trip to London. Obviously this is Chairman Elmis' mission when he is around. Otherwise it is delegated to Caj and always with the same result.

Another fine tradition is that we always walk from our hotel to Loftus Road when QPR play there. Apart from the healthy aspect, there are many opportunities to visit a few pubs along the way. We usually eat lunch at one of the pubs around Shepherd's Bush, where the importance of following traditions are carried on. This is something I myself was made aware of when, ordering a glass of red wine with the pasta I was about to eat. The bar staff and my group did look a bit bemused but they did not in any way refuse to take the order. Everyone got their pints and I got my glass of red. To compare the taste of my red wine with vinegar is not fair – to the vinegar. The taste was terrible, and red wine had most likely not been ordered since around VE-Day. We actually tried to see if Dutta could drink it, but he declined. Usually, he doesn't say no to anything drinkable in a pub. Well, that's how it goes when one tries it on in a pub that most likely does not stock up on their fancy wines, or use it as a marketing tool. I won't order red wine in that pub again, and I left with more conviction to stick to what I know and what is safe. Of course, I have apologised to my friends for this ill-placed attempt at snobbery in a pub in Shepherd's Bush.

If anyone should think that football and beer dominate our trips, I would like to suggest otherwise. Our trips also contain fine culture. One of our days always contains an excursion, preferably somewhere with historical or cultural value. Usually, but not always, this is deemed a success. One of the less successful excursions was when we visited Cambridge and its university grounds. Many of our party felt this to be a bit much culture, while walking around amongst old historical buildings. Caj saw that the group started to lose focus on the culture, with some walking on the nice lawns and not too discretely drinking out of their small bottles of whisky carry outs. One of the group members encountered the lack of toilet facilities and decided to go behind a tree. The trouble was that the tree was a lot thinner than this Viking. Caj realised the problem and said:

Affe, we got it wrong. Our boys are much more practical than theoretical and not very academic by nature. Cambridge University is not the right excursion for this group.

We quickly gathered our party and moved to the nearest pub. It felt good, and the group seemed more focused again.

Apart from this, our excursions are usually very successful. We've been sightseeing along the Thames. We have taken the train to Brighton and walked along the beach in a warm sun in November. We have visited the new and old Wembley Stadium and Warwick outside Birmingham to visit Caj's daughter Åsa who lives here with her husband and two children.

Believe it or not, but we have also visited the Queen's residence in Windsor. Not as invited guests of course, but outside the Castle. After saying goodbye with a regal wave, we went to a pub nearby to eat lunch and have a few pints. Speaking of which, we have also visited St. Albans outside London, and one of the oldest pubs in Britain. We think we are quite good at combining high culture and visiting pubs and see no discrepancies between the two.

During our visit to St. Albans, we feel we made an impression on its inhabitants. At the town square we celebrated that Belle, before departure scored a hole-in-one, by drinking champagne and singing the national anthem. Puzzled onlookers applauded.

Another great episode during one of our excursions was that Caj, in a tube train filled with children aged between 3-5, in full force sang a classic children's hymn in Swedish. He was sober at this time, for it was 10.00 a.m. and we were heading to Brighton. The children's faces were a picture. There was a mix of joy and fear there. We think it all ended well, and when the children stepped off the train with their teachers they were probably convinced the man from Sweden was nice, but most likely also a bit mad.

We are no opportunists, QPR rarely win when we watch them. In Sweden, as well as other countries, supporters of teams like Chelsea and Manchester Untied have grown rapidly over the years. We respect everyone's freedom to express their support and sympathy for any team they like. But can't look away from the obvious opportunism that comes with new supporters of clubs financed by Russian billionaires or dollar hungry media moguls from America. Supporting QPR couldn't be further from opportunism. Unfortunately, it is very rare that our team wins or even gets a share of the points when we watch them. In all honesty, the games with QPR are pretty poor.

One example of that fact that QPR may not be the most entertaining spectacle is when Curre fell asleep during a game against Leicester City. A game that QPR lost 1-2 after a disastrous mistake by the goalkeeper. Curre misses everything, and when we wake him up he says he doesn't want to watch the first team too, after seeing the second team play. He has clearly been dreaming and thinks that one game with QPR is enough. We agree, and help him out of Loftus Road.

When we were in London in 2008, QPR played Ipswich away and of course we wanted to take the train to support our team. The weather was terrible, with heavy rain throughout the day. Unfortunately QPR's game kind of followed suit. The home team won 2-0, and not even we could say that it wasn't fair. We decided to stop in at the pub near the train station, which we had visited before the game. But this day was full of obstacles and the pub was shut so there was nothing else to do but to share the over crowded train back to London with the smell of wet clothes and alcohol. Dutta was in good spirits, engaging in Swedish with English people for most of the journey. It felt good when the train arrived at Liverpool Street Station.

As I mentioned earlier, Caj has transferred his feelings for QPR to his son Niklas. This means that Niklas has seen a lot of QPR games and really knows what it is like to watch your favourite team lose. But when Niklas visited Loftus Road for the 24th time the miracle happened – QPR won 4-2! It was the first time Niklas saw his team win and his tears of joy were very natural. Feel free to criticise our choice of team and games, but you can never call us opportunists.

Since the football at Loftus Road rarely warms our hearts and souls, we have developed a few tricks. One is drinking poor man's Irish coffee. The recipe is very simple – buy a white coffee at Loftus Road, poor a miniature bottle of whisky in it. Done. It usually helps keep the spirits high throughout the game.

Our linguistic problems are a limitation, but there are solutions. It is best to admit it – our knowledge of the English language is not great. This forces us to come up with creative solutions. One of the masters of this newly, invented language is Dutta. When ordering food and drink in pubs and restaurants he simply shadows one of his mates and says...*the same*. The result of this is that Dutta very rarely knows what he has ordered. But in his defence, he never complains about getting the wrong food or drink. He eats, drinks and pays for what he gets.

Despite our linguistic challenges, I have to say that we really try to communicate with other people. Sometimes our hearty approach can backfire. There is one incident with Belle that we all have laughed at since. Late at night we were in London city centre, trying to get back to our hotel in Bayswater. But after a long day and night you get hungry, so before we left we ordered Jumbos with onion and mustard to go. While walking around, eating our Jumbos, a car stops and waves for us to come. It looks like the car passenger wants to ask for directions. The only one stepping towards the car is Belle. The passenger waves for Belle to come a little closer. Belle does so, carrying his Jumbo in one hand. As he gets really close, the passenger sticks his head out of the car and takes a huge bite out of Belle's Jumbo and the car the speeds off. The shock on his face is a picture hard to describe, but it will stay with us forever. It also demonstrates our strong desire to communicate.

We could continue to tell stories and anecdotes from our trips to London. I still hope that we've managed to portray that we have a lot of fun on our trips. What does the future hold? No one knows. As I write this, I am being informed that QPR have sacked a manager once again, and appointed a new manager in Neil Warnock. Will he be our saviour or will we have to take matters into our own hands to set this club straight? Time will tell.

6

Hartlepool United, The FA Cup, Australia and the 2010 South Africa World Cup Final

Musings of a Football Tragic

Denis Pickett

Like many of my generation, I did not see a real football until I was about eleven years old; my first footie-boots (with leather studs) were much later. Growing up in the North-East shipbuilding town of West Hartlepool during the Second World War, sporting equipment did not exist in the extreme rationing conditions. Our knowledge of football was limited to the words of wisdom passed on by our grandfathers and elder uncles and focused more on the exploits of the early 1930s stars such as Dixie Dean and those local stars such as George Hardwick, Wilf Mannion and Raich Carter, whose careers had been interrupted by the war effort.

The football pitches at the local Recreation Ground had been seconded for the duration as an Italian prisoner-of-war camp and our childhood games were therefore restricted to the narrow cobble-stoned lanes separating the rows of terraced houses. Mondays were a 'no-no' being washing days with clothes draped across the lanes on peg-lines and props; similarly Fridays were more a game of dodgem with the coalman delivering sacks of coal on his horse-drawn cart.

Nevertheless, we had some great matches with each terrace fielding a team of five or six kids. No referees or whistles and the rules were very rudimentary – the word 'offside' didn't feature in our vocabulary. The goals were chalked on the end walls and the ball was usually an old pre-war tennis ball or if we were lucky an inflated pig's bladder from the local butchers. Prior to each game we had to clear the pitch of shrapnel and spent machine gun cartridges from the previous night's bombing raid on the nearby dockyards. On one occasion in 1942 we even lost a pitch when an adjoining terrace was almost wiped out by a stray bomb.

I developed a reputation as an attacking forward in the style of a budding Wayne Rooney being very agile on the slippery cobble-stones and becoming adept at passing the opposition by bouncing the ball in the old 'one-two' off the lane side-wall. Unfortunately, these back-lane skills did not transcribe to the full scale in later years when I became, in the old parlance, an attacking left half in the mode, if not quality, of Steven Gerrard.

At the War's end, things got slowly back to normal. The FA leagues restarted, in those days with four divisions, a First, Second and two Thirds (North and South). A two-up and two-down system operated and those teams ending up at the bottom of the Third Divisions had to be re-elected or be replaced by an up and coming team such as Bishop Auckland or Wimbledon. My local team, Hartlepool United, tended to languish in the lower half of the Third Division North but the nearby city teams Middlesbrough, Newcastle and Sunderland lorded it in the First Division. Local derbys were therefore fairly frequent and hard fought.

At the international level, England reigned supreme. They couldn't fail to with a defence line including Frank Swift (goalie), George Hardwick and Neil Franklin; while the forward line of Matthews, Mortenson, Lawton, Mannion and Finney in my view has never been surpassed. Europe was still recovering from the devastation of war and South American teams were still waiting international recognition while the African, Middle East and Asian regions did not then feature on the football map.

Everyone played the 2-3-5 formation and the European/World Cup competitions were yet to re-emerge. The only real challenges to England came from the home countries of Scotland, Ireland and Wales. Televised matches were still a gleam in someone's eye and the fans, unless fortunate enough to get tickets to the big games, had to rely on newspapers, radio and Gaumont News at the cinema to keep up with the exploits of their favourite teams.

All this changed in the early 1950s with the arrival of the Hungarian team lead by the incomparable Puskas; many a tear was shed at England's first loss at Wembley in a 6-3 drubbing. The long-ball game became old-hat overnight, new formations of 4-2-4 and 3-4-3 were tried and Wolverhampton Wanderers under Stan Cullis lead the way into European competition.

Schoolboy competitions took longer to get reorganised and in 1947 I won a scholarship to a college in Middlesbrough which precluded me from participation in after-school games because of the travel distance, time and costs. I therefore became a keen footie spectator. At school this meant that every time there was a mid-week game at Ayresome Park, be it an international or FA Cup replay, we got the afternoon off to attend. As well as keeping up to date with my favourite stars like Wilf Mannion, I also witnessed the emergence of young players like Brian Clough scoring his regular 40 goals per season.

On the home front, I became an avid Hartlepool United (Pools) fan turning up every Saturday afternoon at the Victoria Ground clutching my 6p entrance fee. In those days the ground had a capacity of about 10,000 with 95% of the spectators standing on open mud terraces exposed to the raw North Sea elements. The pitch itself was well maintained and drained quickly due to the sandy substrata. It may have snowed heavily overnight but there were always plenty of loyal fans on hand to clear the pitch so that the match started on schedule at 3.00pm.

Always struggling financially in the lower half of the third division, the club relied on a small squad of part-time players training two days a week (no floodlights in those days) and augmenting their £5 a week from the club with regular jobs. The very survival of the club was due in no small part to the wiles and skills of the manager Fred Westgarth. He was a manager of the old school, shunning publicity but on good terms with his more well-known contemporaries in the higher divisions such as Tom Whittaker of Arsenal, Matt Busby of Manchester United and Bill Shankly of Liverpool. Fred was often given the opportunity to sign up, at a minimal transfer fee, a player not quite reaching the top division standards or nearing the end of his career; while the Pools' Board made sure that suitable part-time employment was available.

Fred's strength was his ability to build a team from a blend of these mature players and young locals with potential. Springing to mind are the likes of Watty Moore, a consummate centre-half but too short in stature for the top divisions, and a local lad Leo Harden, often the butt of the crowd but every so often producing that touch of left wing magic. In later years, some of my contemporaries in the district competition earned a guernsey, several moving on to higher levels at a decent transfer fee; another 'earner' for the club as the players in those days only received the glory but no part of the transfer money.

Assisting Fred was his younger brother Ned, the trainer. The sight of Ned lumbering across the field with his bag of potients, lotions and smelling salts in one hand while carrying a bucket of icy water and sponge in the other was enough to get most players back on their feet long before a puffing Ned arrived. Some great characters! In later years, a worthy successor to Fred was a young Brian Clough. This was his first managerial role before he moved on to greater fame with Derby County and Nottingham Forest.

Although lacking consistency in the league competition, Pools developed a reputation as gritty cup fighters often reaching the fourth or fifth round. The financial incentive was the sharing of the gate proceeds when an away draw with a first division team was in the offing. On one famous occasion, Pools were drawn to play at home to the Manchester United 'Busby Babes'. There was talk of moving the game to Old Trafford but in the end loyalty to the faithful Pools' supporters was given priority.

The ground was packed an hour before the match started and I was one of the lucky ones to be there. It was a fast attacking game and Pools were not disgraced, holding their own for the first 45 minutes, but in the end superior fitness and finesse prevailed and the Babes ran out winners by a comfortable margin. The match is still talked about in Hartlepool with a touch of reverence and awe.

One of the Babes was an 18 year old Duncan Edwards. This was the second time I'd seen him play; a couple of years earlier he had played at the Victoria Ground in a youth representative game. The third and last time was his international debut against Scotland during my first visit to the 120,000 cauldron of Hampden Park. I shall never forget his dominance of the game with his uncanny balance and deft footwork for such a large player and his ability to split a defence with long, fast and accurate on-the-ground passes. His death with many of his Babe team-mates in the Munich air disaster was an inestimable loss to football.

By this time, I had started to venture further afield in my spectator role whenever there was a league derby or cup-tie between the northeast city teams; watching the goal-scoring exploits of the great Jackie Milburn at St James' Park or the dazzling talents of Len Shackleton at Roker Park. On one memorable occasion, I had been to a match at Middlesbrough with my father. After the game we were walking with the crowd to travel across the famous Transporter Bridge and catch a bus home, my father searching the late edition of the local paper for the outcome of his betting selection on the Littlewood Pools.

He already had seven draws and was sweating on a late starting game at Hull. There it was in black and white, a one-nil win to the home team. Worse still, the goal had been scored in the final minute and there were only nine draws that weekend. Henceforth he was called 'Happy Harry' because his party piece every Christmas after a few drinks was to narrate how he nearly made his fortune on the pools; we never dared mention Hull in his presence again!

I started playing competitive football when I entered the workforce as an apprentice ship designer at the local shipyard, initially in an under eighteen team then at the senior district level. This encompassed playing at most of the regional pit villages. All hard but clean games; the greatest difficulty was understanding the local dialect. Serious injuries were few, mainly bruised shins and twisted ankles; none of the ankle clipping tackles, physical man-handling in the penalty area or the theatrical diving of the modern era. At the end of the game we would all shake hands and return together to the clubhouse for a few celebration pints of Camerons' Best or Newcastle Brown Ale before trundling home on the char-a-banc.

Every season we joined the many amateur teams playing in the preliminary rounds of the FA Cup. One year, we even vied for a Third Round place with the senior professional teams only to be knocked out by a semi-professional Stockton. A fairly close game and we had our chances but eventually went down 2-0 to a fitter and more skilful combination. Equally important from my point of view was that the participation in the cup competition entitled the club to a few FA Cup Final tickets at the end of each season. By then, I was courting a Hartlepool lass who had moved down to Wembley with her family. For eight years I had the pleasure of a weekend visit to the 'big smoke' in May to see the Final and enjoy a convivial evening at a West-end cinema, all with some lovely family accommodation thrown in!

Marching down the concourse to the old Wembley Stadium, then joining the excited 90,000 spectators in the pre-match singing accompanied by the Guards Band, the match itself and the post-match medal presentations fused together in an unforgettable experience. Although each game was different in character and style, each was played in a typical cup-final spirit, if not always in a classic football sense.

One game that sticks in my mind was the year of the Munich air disaster when a cobbled-together Manchester United (assisted by the goodwill transfers of key players from other clubs) reached the final under the guidance of the stand-in manager Jimmy Murphy. Along with 90% of the crowd I was willing Manchester to win but it was not to be, United going down 1-0 to the scoring power of Bolton's Nat Lofthouse. It would be a few years before Matt Busby was able to rebuild the team to its previous status with the addition of new stars such as George Best, Dennis Law and Nobby Stiles; and the world-class skills of Bobby Charlton finally reached fruition.

Called up for two-years National Service in 1959, my competitive football changed focus to inter-regiment and inter-forces games; a great relief from the daily grind of square-bashing, barracks-cleaning and battle-field exercises. In retrospect, it proved to be a valuable character building experience, particularly the 12 months overseas posting to Kenya at the tail end of the Mau Mau insurrection. After the necessary acclimatization at 3000 feet, I continued my services football; some of the hardest games being against the Ascaris of the Kings African Rifles who played in barefeet on the rock-hard ground.

On returning to civvy street, I continued to play but at the more relaxed village level, having moved to Essex on a new ship research job and married the Hartlepool lass. However, age started to catch up and it took longer to recover from even the slightest footie injury. With the onset of family responsibilities I decided to retire gracefully and become one of the original 'couch potato' spectators. By then, major matches were being televised live in black and white, reaching a pinnacle during the 1966 World Cup tournament.

Whether it was the picnic atmosphere, with friends crowded round the 17" set supping their beers, but every England game in that series seemed fast and exciting. Alf Ramsey, a former international, a players' manager and a master tactician, had put together a real team squad. The players knew that Alf would go out on a limb to support them and they in turn gave him their full loyalty and endeavours. With players of the calibre of Gordon Banks, Bobby Moore, Nobby Stiles, Martin Peters, Geoff Hurst and the incomparable Bobby Charlton, the squad was flexible enough to meet every match situation. Who could forget the see-sawing final with Germany!

Unfortunately, England has never been able to reach the same heights again. Things may have been different if Brian Clough had been chosen to replace Alf Ramsey but Cloughie was out of favour with the establishment, despite being in the same mould as Alf and the leading manager of his day. The only worthy modern day equivalent is Harry Redknapp but it remains to be seen whether the powers-that-be will make the right choice this time and put proven success ahead of their perceptions of social niceties.

In late 1969, I moved with my family to Australia on a defence contract in Canberra. To say it was a culture shock in football terms is an understatement. Four football codes are played, the ubiquitous Aussie Rules, both forms of rugby and soccer. On my first parent/teacher night, a volunteer was required to coach the school's junior football team. Naturally my hand went up and for the next five months I found myself running up and down the pitch with a rule book in my hand (coaches were allowed on the field at this level) trying to encourage the boys on the finer points of Aussie Rules!

The pitch is oval and much larger than in soccer or rugby with four goalposts at each end; the ball is also an elongated oval shape designed for hand-marking as much as kicking. There are eighteen players per side and five controlling officials called umpires. I won't dwell on the unique terminology but when I say Aussie Rules I mean 'rules'. Interpreting the rule book is a bureaucrat's seventh heaven and the book seems to be rewritten every year! Don't get me wrong; I enjoy watching the game on TV and have even attended a grand final at the MCG but soccer is still my one true (football) love.

Recovering from this initial coaching trauma, I resolved that henceforth when I meant the world game of football I would need to use the word 'soccer' in my adopted country. Australia has the potential to become a great soccer nation. Its youth is generally tall and athletic with natural ball skills, as demonstrated by the country's successes in the international arenas of rugby, cricket, tennis, golf and hockey. However, the population is relatively small and soccer until recently has been the poor relation in terms of sport. What was needed was a youth development programme, a national league and as much international competition as possible. All of these goals have been achieved, albeit with the need for further improvements. The success of these initiatives was demonstrated in the 2006 World Cup when Australia reached Round 16, only to be defeated by the Aussie equivalent of 'the hand of God', the infamous Italian dive to claim a last minute penalty.

Aussie Rules is still the dominant football sport in Australia but with the advent of world-wide live colour TV transmissions via satellite there is a growing audience of soccer 'couch potatoes'. Since settling in the Western Australian city of Perth, and putting to rest my small contributions to junior soccer coaching and refereeing, I have joined these soccer tragics, focusing in particular on the English football scene. I now have no favourite players or clubs but simply enjoy the game as a neutral, viewing events from a remote distance. The following comments should therefore be read in this context.

I have watched with interest and support the changing FA league structure, going from a four division tier arrangement to three divisions plus the Premier League. This has resulted in many positives but a number of disturbing problems have emerged with the Premier League's dependence on outside sponsorships and money interests.

Player remunerations and contractual arrangements have improved dramatically from the bad old days when a professional player was totally owned by the club on a fixed maximum weekly wage of £12 with no rights of transfer; receiving only a £10 fee from say a £20,000 exchange between the clubs for a top class player. I wonder whether the modern players appreciate the career sacrifices of the original rebel to this unfair practice, Wilf Mannion, or the negotiating efforts of Jimmy Hill on behalf of the players union to improve the situation. Unfortunately, things are now starting to get out of hand with players earning more in a month than the average loyal fan earns in a lifetime!

Transfer fees are escalating in the tens of millions with the player receiving a significant component; thus transfers are frequent with an overseas player's tenure with one club being typically two years. Examples of the traditional one-club player, such as Ryan Giggs or Paul Scholes, are few and club loyalty is compromised.

To fund these excessive contract and transfer costs, the clubs have to rely on sponsorships to supplement the income from television rights while gate takings are becoming an ever smaller component of club income, despite the entrance charges now being beyond the paying capacity of the average family of a father and two sons. To maintain the status to attract sponsorship and TV support, the clubs scour the world for the best managers and players. Quite often the top clubs such as Arsenal and Chelsea will field teams with only one homegrown player!

It's an ever vicious cycle where the FA has lost control of the Premier League to the TV moguls and international sponsors; clubs are getting themselves into bankruptcy situations with the traditional club board and supporters' organizations being superseded as clubs become the investment playthings of Russian or American billionaires. Much emphasis is placed on performing in the European Champions League such that the old FA Cup (or whatever the current sponsorship name is) is fast becoming a minor event at the end of the season.

On a positive note, the imported players and managers have certainly helped raise the footballing standards. Players are super fit, often playing two matches a week, and ball control skills are at an all-time high. Even the goalkeeper is expected to participate in the backline passing interchanges before the lightning-fast switch to offence, while fullbacks frequently overlap as attacking wingers. It all makes for exciting and attractive end-to-end football.

The changes in the league structures and operations have also affected the performances of the England team. Players act and are treated like 'prima donnas' making team blending difficult. Moreover, the large influx of overseas players prevents homegrown players accessing the upper levels of the Premier League, resulting in a much more limited selection pool of international class talent. Hopefully this situation will improve if the proposal, to enforce a minimum content of (say) 20% homegrown players in each Premier League squad, is adopted.

However, ever the optimist, I have high hopes that these English league problems will be redressed to the betterment of football. It is a great world game with the ability to bring people together from diverse financial and racial backgrounds, where so-called Third World countries are on an equal footing with the most advanced nations on the planet. This view was reinforced with startling effect during my recent visit to South Africa for the 2010 World Cup Final.

The opportunity was broached to me by one of my sons during a fishing trip on the abundant coastal waters off Perth. He had the option to purchase two tickets and the proposal was that my extended family would fully cover my trip to the tournament accompanied by another son, whom I dubbed 'Moses Matt' because he was to lead the way and keep me on the straight and narrow! Initially I demurred because my last visit to Johannesburg had been in 1966 in the midst of the terrible apartheid regime but after some persuasion I agreed to go; it was one of the best decisions I have made. I'm still recovering from the euphoria of experiencing such a colourful and friendly event.

Our base for the five-day trip was the Protea Hotel situated in the grounds of the famous Wanderers Club, the national sport and social centre for rugby, cricket, squash etc. Being hotel residents also entitled us to temporary membership of the magnificent colonial-style clubhouse and we made full use of the facilities including the bar and large TV screens. Through the benefits of satellite transmissions, we were able to watch an All Blacks v Springboks rugby test match from New Zealand one morning and the third-place World Cup football match from Port Elizabeth the same evening.

Between times we did the touristy thing, using public transport and 'shanks pony' where possible, visiting the local zoo to see the unique pride of white lions, shopping for vuvuzelas (a parent's delight) and enjoying the city's top class restaurant scene with the many overseas supporters wearing their national colours. Most noticeable everywhere we went was the warm welcoming atmosphere from the locals and visitors alike, of whatever persuasion, colour or creed. I've never encountered in my 74 years a real coming together of the world's humanity and potential for peace as stimulated by this great tournament of football.

Then came cup-final day with a backdrop of clear blue skies, no wind and the temperature hovering around the 18°C mark. We left the hotel early because of the 15km journey to the new 'Soccer City Stadium' in Soweto and the uncertainty of how the transport, security and entrance systems would work in getting the 90,000 spectators into and out of the ground. In the event everything went like clockwork; access routes and freeways were closed to all traffic except trains and coaches, with hundreds of designated pickup points dotted around the city. Ours was only 200m from the hotel, very useful when we returned at 2.30am!

I won't try to describe the spectacle of the crowds, the ceremonies or the match, you've seen it all on television. Suffice to say that we were simply part of a magical event. Though fast and furious, the game did not live up to the high football expectations with Spain (the eventual worthy winners) trying to play attractive football and the Netherlands bent on winning a trophy at any cost. The most disturbing aspect for me was the continuous confrontation with the referee, every decision was challenged and diving was taken to a fine art with the clear intention of getting an opponent red-carded. In a normal game at least two players would have been sent off before half-time and at the final whistle several Dutch players had to be physically restrained from virtually attacking the referee. Such antics have to be stamped out.

Departure day and how to fill-in the eight hour gap before our flight home? 'Moses Matt' had the brilliant idea of visiting the Apartheid Museum, the most moving experience of our visit. The exhibition describes the development of a great nation from the centuries of colonial domination with their slavery and segregation laws, through the three decades of the horrendous apartheid regime which commenced in the early 1950s, to the establishment of a democratic republic in the 1990s with a written constitution guaranteeing freedom and human rights for all South Africans.

A special section in the exhibition depicts the life of Nelson Mandela who was at the core of anti-apartheid movement and still wields enormous influence in the current post reconciliation period. A highlight of the World Cup closing ceremony was to witness the standing ovation given to this aging but great orator, charismatic leader and international statesman.

We spent five hours at the museum and could have stayed another five. The soccer-mad Venezuelan lady, who shared our taxi to the airport, had delayed her departure from this her fifth World Cup series to visit the exhibition three times. She was already talking about a rendezvous in 2014 but I have a feeling this will be vetoed by my family who consider the Rio World Cup would prove far too exciting for a then 78 year old geriatric with thirteen grandchildren. Nevertheless, I live in hope and my greatest hope is that the England management and team will finally get their act together by then!

7

Perth Glory

Gloree Days

Alex Alexandrou

Gloree!! Gloree!! Gloree!!

These were the hypnotic words that greeted me upon my arrival at the Perth Oval as part of my initiation into Aussie life as part of what would turn out to be a memorable long winter holiday covering the last days of 1996 and the early days of 1997. It was also well into the Australian football (soccer) season. The purpose of my visit was to pay homage to the "shrine" named "The Shed". This is where the "boys" of Perth sang the praises of their one and only Perth Glory every other Saturday.

For the uninitiated, Perth Glory were back then a recently constituted club that had been set up to challenge the dominance of the teams from the east of the country where predominantly all the football had been played for many decades; and to break down the racial barriers that had for so long afflicted the great game in Australia, again because of being played on the east coast of the nation where the racial divide between those of Greek, Italian, Serb, Croat and Turkish origin was as hostile as we now see in many parts of Europe. This east coast dominance had significantly hindered the development of Australian football in terms of it becoming a power in the world game.

I had only been in Perth a week but had been instructed in the rites of the Saturday afternoon by new found and not so new friends. I was informed that football as I knew it was alive and kicking in this most remote of state capital cities and had a team of upstarts more than capable of challenging the east coast established order. By the time I had arrived "Gloree" were already fourth in the league and had just annihilated the pre-season favourites Brisbane 5-1 on their own manor.

What drew me to watch Perth play against the Woolagong Wolves (as if I needed any encouragement) was the reputation of the home team's fans. British ex-pats and those on a long vacation from Blighty had taken over one part of the ground and were showing the growing band of Aussie converts what being a football fan was all about. I was intrigued because at the time, back home my experiences of going to matches around England were not great to say the least. I went to the game expecting to be surrounded and herded about by unforgiving police officers, fed up that they were partaking in another Saturday punch-up; unable to get a drink because the pubs were shut; rival fans being segregated and that we would have to sit. Wrong on all counts and well off the mark!

The crew I was going with were all Aussies and well up for a day's adventure. We met up in the morning, many hours before kick-off and were soon into the swing of things as the boys insisted that we stopped off at the bottle shop (off-licence to you and I in the UK) to stock up on a few tinnies to get us through our journey! Which bemused me as Perth was not that big a city. The initial supplies were disposed of with admirable ease and the tone for the day was set. To my amazement we were able to park up (that is the unfortunate driver who drew the short straw) right near the ground with no bother and the best was yet to come.

It was a warm, sunny day in December; there were no police, or so few that it made no odds; no segregation; just a few security guards to watch over things; it was in those days only $10, which equated to £5 to get in and a couple of dollars for the match programme. Then there was a sight for sore eyes – a terrace where you could stand (which had become no longer possible, if like me you supported a Premier League team back in England) and a shack next to it where you could purchase any amount of tinnies before, during and after the game. Heaven for one fed up to the back teeth of not being able to enjoy a few pints on a Saturday while paying a pilgrimage to their chosen team.

Supplies were purchased and the order of who went up to get the next round during the next two hours was sorted out in a vaguely hazy democratic manner. We found a decent spot at the back of the terrace and were greeted with the first rendition of "Gloree Gloree". The stand soon filled up and there must have been about 5,000 of us, most of whom were sporting their team colours from back home. These ranged from the usual Man Utd, Liverpool, Spurs and Arsenal to the likes of Millwall, Reading and Southend. There were plenty of boys (not many women there but that should be no surprise) sporting the Glory's kit but you wouldn't get me wearing the home top which was sponsored by one of the local chicken fast food joints. Corporate sponsorship was yet to hit the Glory!

The crescendo of noise rose rapidly as the stand filled up. The buzz was there fuelled by all the songs once sang with full gusto at the grounds back home but sadly and crushingly being destroyed by the advent of all-seater stadiums where demure middle-class families were being chased for their cash rather than those for whom football was part of the social fabric of their community and was part of their very being. I detected a certain bias towards a scouse theme song about walking alone and a rabid hatred of all things United (Manchester of course!). What a difference this was to the previous week, when on a cold grey Saturday afternoon, I had been to watch in almost near silence Manchester United take on Leicester City and although they won, a young Emile Heskey bullied, battered and bruised the Reds' defence that many saw him as a future England international. They were right but where was the Heskey of old in South Africa?

I was loving every minute of it and getting hoarse as I had not done for a long while despite the ample supply of the amber nectar. We sang, we danced, we took the piss and saluted our hero "Sloppy Bobby". This was Perth's top man up front, who on numerous occasions misdirected his thunderbolts in our direction but still did the business. We couldn't out sing the opposition, because there were none but we stayed on for an hour after the game to give it our all and dance the obligatory conga, setting us up nicely for an evening's continued imbibing and partying.

Oh, by the way, "The Gloree" won 3-1.

8

Ipswich Town

Bees, Blues and Tractor Boys

Peter Simkins

Unlike many lads, I didn't inherit a football team from my Dad. He didn't even take me to my first game. I think it was our next-door neighbour in Greenford, Middlesex, who took me to Stamford Bridge, in the 1946-1947 season, to see Chelsea play Sheffield United. I have vague memories of Harry Medhurst and Tommy Walker playing for Chelsea and a somewhat over-robust red-haired Scotsman – Alex Forbes (an early prototype of Billy Bremner) – appearing for the Blades. Coincidentally, one of Chelsea's stars of that era, Len Goulden, became a near-neighbour of ours when we moved to Wealdstone a decade or so later. My Dad, who quite liked watching football but was never truly grabbed by it, *did* take me to my second game, in February 1948, when Brentford beat Bury 8-2 at Griffin Park. Again, I have hazy recollections of Peter McKennan scoring five for the Bees, and also of the disconcertingly bald Brentford full back, Bill Gorman, who, apparently, was known as 'Old Naked Brains'. This was still in the days of heavy leather footballs with laces that stung your thighs, huge boots and studs which could inflict mortal injuries, and goalkeepers who wore thick wool roll-neck jerseys and flat caps. Indeed, there was far more material in the average centre-half's shorts than there was in my entire childhood wardrobe in that era of Austerity.

Living where I did in Greenford, I had the choice, when growing up into my teens, of watching at least four different league clubs. I was, in truth, a fickle lover, never really getting passionate about any one potential object of my affection but flirting unashamedly with each in turn. My Mum, God bless her, came with me just once on the 105 bus for my first-ever visit to Loftus Road to see QPR in action in the days when

Ron Springett was in goal. I returned to Chelsea on occasion, particularly during the season when, with the admirable Roy Bentley leading the forward line, they finally shrugged off their nickname of 'Pensioners' and landed the old First Division Championship. I was, in turn, hugely impressed by the fact that Fulham sent me, on request, the autographs of all their current players, so, for a while, I paid court to the residents of Craven Cottage, who then included the wonderful Johnny Haynes and that unique amalgam of hero and clown, Tosh Chamberlain. However, it was Brentford who probably exerted the strongest pull on me. I watched them fairly regularly when the team included Ron Greenwood, Bill Slater, the ungainly Jimmy Hill and the legendary Tommy Lawton – then well past his peak but still capable of scoring sensational headed goals which I can still see in my mind's eye.

One Saturday at Griffin Park, almost certainly in 1952, a movie company shot part of a football-based film called 'The Great Game', starring James Hayter, Thora Hird and Diana Dors. One of the crowd's tasks, as unpaid extras, was to cheer loudly when a couple of rather effete actors emerged from the tunnel wearing the Brentford strip. Far more appealing was the fact that, in our section of the ground, the British screen siren, Diana Dors, had to pretend to faint near the back of the terrace, then allow herself to be passed down horizontally over the heads of the crowd onto the pitch for 'medical attention'. At that time, I was far too young to fully appreciate, or seize, this unrivalled opportunity to grab a handful of Miss Dors' ample flesh, but I could be seen, loyally wearing my school cap, in a photograph which was taken that afternoon and which duly appeared the following week in the *Middlesex County Times*.

The nearest I came to declaring undying love for a West London team was in the 1957-1958 season, when Brentford narrowly missed promotion to Division Two. My younger brother Geoff and I saw many of the home fixtures at Griffin Park in that exciting season and, over fifty years later, I can still name the regular starting line-up: Cakebread, Wilson, Horne, Bristow, Dargie, Coote, Parsons, Rainford, Francis, Towers and Newcombe. The twin strikers, Jim Towers and George Francis, scored 52 goals between them that term. Having just beaten Brighton and Hove Albion 1-0, the Bees were pipped to promotion by Brighton themselves a couple of days later, when the Albion scored six in a match against Watford which allegedly involved bribery. I could not forgive Brighton for that season's disappointments, though guess where the family ended up when we moved south in 1961. You've got it in one......Brighton!!

I lived very happily in Brighton for twenty-two years but, perhaps still bearing a grudge, I never had any genuine affection for the Albion, or the Seagulls as they subsequently became known – not even when they reached the dizzy heights of Division One or the Cup Final at Wembley ('...and Smith *must* score'!). Although I went to the old Goldstone Ground two or three times each season and enjoyed watching players like Mark Lawrenson, Steve Foster, Peter Ward, Michael Robinson and the vastly-underrated wing-half Jack Bertolini, I'm sorry to say that I even developed a perverse pleasure in seeing the team lose. Perhaps it was because, during those years by the seaside, my sporting affections were largely focused upon Sussex County Cricket Club (of which I became a Member) and the Brighton Tigers ice hockey team. Even so, despite these new loves, I was uncomfortably aware that, until a football club won my heart, there would always be something missing in my otherwise very full life.

It was in the early 1970s that I first began to experience that tingling feeling in one's football loins that signals 'This is the one!' I cannot precisely identify the date but I do know that, as a result of seeing them regularly on *Match of the Day* or *The Big Match*, I became singularly attracted to the brand of football being played by Ipswich Town under Bobby Robson. The fact that a relatively unglamorous and unfashionable side from East Anglia was now clearly capable of matching the likes of Manchester United and Arsenal in both style and substance made them all the more appealing to me – even if the only time I had ever been near the place was in the late 1950s when the jazz group I then played for used to stop overnight in the town with our Ipswich-born drummer's parents after late gigs at the nearby American air bases at Bentwaters and Woodbridge. I was also aware, of course, that Ipswich had achieved the amazing feat of actually winning the Division One title, under Alf Ramsey, in 1961-1962.

From the televised highlights on *Match of the Day* in the 1970s, I recall, in particular, majestic headed goals by Trevor Whymark. Glossing swiftly over the uncomfortable fact that he had the bad luck to be born in bandit country (Norfolk), I'm sure that I am not alone in rating Whymark as one of the very best home-grown East Anglian footballers ever to grace Portman Road – and there have been a good few of those over the years. That Whymark was only awarded one full England cap (as a substitute against lowly Luxembourg in 1978) is nothing short of scandalous. I also vividly remember a tremendous goal scored by the truly great Kevin Beattie in a 4-1 win against West Ham in April 1975, when he sliced through the Hammers' defence with the power of a Tiger tank and the balance and agility of Nijinsky. The Ipswich side of those days was full of outstanding characters and fine footballers, with the elegant George Burley and the gritty captain Mick Mills as full (wing) backs. In front of them were the powerful Brian Talbot (an Ipswich-born lad), the no-nonsense Allan Hunter and Kevin Beattie, and other splendid players included the South African Colin Viljoen, Bryan Hamilton, David Johnson (the Mark I variant), Mick Lambert, and the skilful (and uncapped) Clive Woods, also an escapee from neighbouring Norfolk. Between the posts from 1974 onwards was the supreme penalty-stopper, Paul Cooper.

To this tasty mix was added, in October 1976, Paul Mariner, who joined Town from Plymouth for £220,000 in what, in retrospect, was one of the bargains of the century. The long-haired, lanky Mariner has been described by local sports writer Tony Garnett as 'one of the most effective hold-up players in England' and arguably 'the classiest centre-forward Ipswich have had on their books'. It was even more encouraging to reflect that an exciting crop of youngsters was emerging from the youth team and reserves during those years. Alan Brazil, Terry Butcher, Eric Gates, David Geddis, Steve McCall, Roger Osborne, Russell Osman, and the magnificent John Wark were all signed as juniors or apprentices, thanks to Town's excellent scouting system.

I trust that my friend, academic colleague and Gunners fan Gary Sheffield will forgive me if I wallow in the memory of two terrific performances against Arsenal in the late 1970s. The first was in April 1977, when Brian Talbot, Kevin Beattie, Keith Bertschin and John Wark scored in a 4-1 triumph over the Gunners at Highbury. This was in the same season that Town thrashed the Baggies 7-0 at Portman Road, with Trevor Whymark scoring four. The second memorable victory over Arsenal was, of course, in the 1978 Cup Final at Wembley. Glued to my television in Brighton, roaring my adopted team on from afar, I witnessed Clive Woods repeatedly turning Pat Rice inside-out, and Mariner and Wark hitting the woodwork three times between them before, in the 77th minute, Willie Young could only divert a David Geddis cross into Suffolk-born Roger Osborne's path and the latter notched the only goal of the game. A marvellous day indeed!

Things got even better as Bobby Robson shrewdly added Dutchmen Arnold Muhren and Frans Thijssen to the squad. Murhen's sweet left foot and Thijssen's mazy dribbling gave an extra dimension to the cultured and flowing football for which Town were renowned in the late 1970s and early 1980s. The chase for further honours culminated in the 1980-1981 season when, at one stage, Ipswich had a good chance of winning the Championship, the FA Cup and the UEFA Cup. In the event, the club's small squad and injuries at key times prevented them from winning all three trophies. Town were runners-up in Division One to Aston Villa, a team they had beaten three times that season, and were knocked out of the FA Cup in the semi-final by Manchester City, but winning the UEFA Cup in Amsterdam went a long way towards compensating supporters for their recent disappointments. On the way to the trophy,

Town achieved a superb 4-1 win away to Michel Platini's St. Etienne side. In the two-leg final against AZ Alkmaar, Town almost threw away a 3-0 lead which they had secured at home, but they held on to win 5-4 on aggregate. During that heady season, the mighty John Wark scored 36 goals *from midfield*, 14 of them in Europe. Imagine what he would be worth on today's inflated transfer market! In my view, despite their near-misses in the League and FA Cup, the stylish 'Boys of '81', as they are still called, were the best team ever put together at Portman Road.

Two years later I actually moved to the town. House-hunting in East Anglia, where property prices were then comparatively cheap, I took a chance, on the advice of a Friday-evening commuter, and stopped overnight in Ipswich and, by 9.30 am next morning, had put in a provisional offer for the house where I was to live with my family for the next two decades or so. It was only when walking back into the town centre for an early beer before catching the train, that I realised, to my delight, that our future home was a mere ten minutes' casual stroll from the hallowed turf of Portman Road. In fact I could even see the floodlight towers and the roof of one of the stands from our bedroom window. I wasted little time in becoming – at last – a season-ticket holder at Portman Road for the 1983-1984 season. The first three home games saw Town beat Spurs 3-1, Everton 3-0 and Stoke 5-0. In the latter game, George Burley, Eric Gates, Paul Mariner and John Wark (2) all got on the scoresheet. Mariner's goal came at the end of one of the most flowing moves I had ever seen in 35 years of watching live football (as distinct from seeing it on the TV). "This'll do me!" I said to our daughter Cathy, who was watching her very first live football match, though, to be honest, on that afternoon *she* seemed more fascinated by the little men jumping up and down on the electronic scoreboard whenever Town hit the back of the net.

Perhaps, in view of my innate sporting pessimism, I should have sensed what was in store, but my arrival as a live fan at Portman Road coincided almost precisely with the start of the club's decline, and it all went steadily downhill from that point! Over the previous eleven seasons, Town had only twice been outside the top six of Division One and had played in Europe in eight of those seasons. In my first campaigns as a season-ticket holder, they were 12th and 17th and were then relegated. Bobby Robson had left for the England manager's job in 1982 and during my first *regular* season the great Mariner and Wark respectively departed for Arsenal and Liverpool. The newly-completed Pioneer Stand was already proving top be a huge financial millstone and I soon learned, reluctantly, to accept the *real* constant factors of being a Town supporter: (a) the club is likely to be relegated, promoted or win a trophy once a decade; (b) the club will continue to hover on the brink of financial meltdown and/or administration but, despite this, will usually tend to exacerbate the problem by building new grandstands or refurbishing old ones; (c) in an effort to ease such financial headaches (where *does* all the revenue go?) the club will repeatedly sell its top players for bargain prices; (d) the club will continue to discover and produce outstanding youngsters who will lift our spirits for a couple of seasons before going to bigger clubs; (e) Town will normally be expected to lose penalty shoot-outs; and (f) whoever is in the team, they will hit the left-hand post at the North Stand (now the Sir Bobby Robson Stand) end at key moments in crucial games.

Paradoxically, as the club sank into Division Two mediocrity, my masochistic loyalty to it intensified, and the volume of my vocal support increased in direct proportion. In his marvellous book *Fatty Batter*, my actor/writer brother Michael describes me as a man 'revered for the balance and discretion of his opinions' who, given a disputed penalty at Portman Road, 'becomes King Kong'. It goes without saying that referees were fair game, but the particular targets of my frequent abuse were, and are, linesmen – I refuse to call them 'referee's assistants' – whose general grasp of the offside rule seemed, on the whole, to be even more tenuous than mine. For most of the period from 1985 to 1995 I sat in the Portman Stand next to a lovely old chap called 'Chalky' White, who had been watching Town since the Kaiser was a lad. In front of us at every home game were four miserable sods who *never* clapped a Town goal, slagged off the referee or expressed any opinion whatsoever. All my attempts to engage them in conversation about the game, the prospects of the club or the meaning of life were met with monosyllabic grunts. When 'Chalky' fell ill and passed on, I changed my habits and switched to the opposite side of the ground, purchasing a season ticket in the Pioneer Stand (Block G, Row I, Seat No.44). Here I found myself surrounded by more congenial fellow-supporters, who were at least prepared to turn a deaf ear to my minute-by-minute ravings!

Miraculously, only once did I come close to being ejected from the ground. This was on a bitterly cold day in the early 2000s when (I think) we were playing Chelsea. To keep out the cold – it's my story and I'm sticking to it – I filled a miniscule hip flask with single malt whisky and had an occasional medicinal sip during the first-half. Apparently the security cameras spotted me and, at half time, I was escorted to a quiet corner by the stewards, who gave me a verbal roasting. However, they recognised me as a loyal and regular supporter and let me off with a caution. What upset me most was that my seat was two rows in front of a corporate hospitality box in which a bunch of complete pillocks, who would probably never be seen at the ground again, got seriously bladdered on Chardonnay, lager and champagne while watching all of two minutes of the game! Most of them, while still upright, seemed more interested in the racing being featured on the television set deep within the hospitality box. For my part, I covertly continued to take my hip flask to matches but just became a little more circumspect in raising it to my lips. God knows, I often need a drop of the hard stuff to preserve my equanimity when watching the once-mighty Town struggle to overcome teams like Crewe, Swindon and Southend. Very occasionally, during matches against top sides such as Manchester United or Liverpool, when the ground was full of people who attended one game every ten years, one of these fair-weather fans would accuse me of being too loud in my opinions. To them my invariable response was: 'When you've sat here on a freezing January night watching a Carling Cup tie against Rochdale, you can tell me to shut up. Until then, you can buzz off!' (or words to that effect).

The frustration and disappointments of the second half of the 1980s – not least the period when John Duncan was manager – were, of course, relieved every so often by the signing of decent players and, in the Ipswich tradition, by the emergence of promising home-grown youngsters. Some of the better imports I still fondly remember from that time include the whippet-like Kevin 'Jocky' Wilson (49 goals in 121 starts) and the somewhat frail-looking David Lowe (42 goals in 144 starts).

I was there for the much-publicised arrival of Ukrainian Sergei Baltacha, who scored on his home debut against Stoke in 1989, but who, despite his popularity with the fans, only made 24 starts and was never played in his specialist position of sweeper. Others who became firm favourites were Dutch midfielder Romeo Zondervan, defender Neil Thompson (who took fine free kicks and corners), and Hartlepool-born central defender David Linighan. Town's fortunes always tend to flourish when they have a big, old-fashioned, no-nonsense centre-half at the club and 'Lini' was a worthy successor to Allan Hunter and Terry Butcher and predecessor of Tony Mowbray.

However, the greatest tonic in indifferent years was the regular introduction of gifted local footballers, apprentices and youth team graduates who cost the club little or nothing. The best of those who made their debut in the 1980s were Ian Cranson and Mark Brennan(1983), Jason Dozzell (1984), Mick Stockwell (1985), Dalian Atkinson and Tony Humes (1986), Simon Milton (1987), and Craig Forrest and Chris Kiwomya (1988). I can clearly recall Jason Dozzell – who was then at the same local High School as our daughter – coming on against Coventry and netting in the 89th minute, at the age of 16 years and 57 days, making him, at that time, the youngest player ever to score a goal in the then First Division. He went on to score 70 more in over 400 appearances for Town. Mick Stockwell too was a splendid servant to the club. He spent 19 years at Portman Road and made over 600 appearances for the first team between 1985 and 2000. However, by no means all of Town's acquisitions in the late 1980s were successes. It has to be said that the likes of David Hill, Glenn Pennyfather, Neil Woods and Graham Harbey seemed pretty lightweight to fans who, but a few years before, had been watching Muhren, Mariner and Brazil.

To be fair to John Duncan, he did have the good sense to re-sign John Wark from Liverpool and help assemble the nucleus of the squad which, under the wily and amiable John Lyall, won the Second Division championship in 1991-1992 and thus entered the brand-new Premier League. At the end of this promotion season, I invaded the pitch for the first and only time in my life (I couldn't get over the barriers now) – along with the majority of the crowd. There were some memorable moments in 1992-1993, including a 4-2 home win against reigning champions Leeds and a 2-0 away win over arch-rivals Norwich City, and there were new heroes to cheer, such as Bulgarian striker Bontcho Guentchev. Nevertheless, one must concede that, with the club's limited resources both on and off the field, Town's initial seasons in the Premiership – leading to almost inevitable relegation in 1995 – was hard going for much of the time. One got a bit tired of journalists and mates at work referring to Town's 'flat back ten', while Leeds manager Howard Wilkinson complained that playing against Ipswich was 'like pushing custard up a hill'.

As in the 1980s, new signings did something to alleviate the almost tangible sense of anti-climax. Ian Marshall and Paul Mason in 1993 were followed by the Dane Claus Thomsen and Argentinian Mauricio Taricco in 1994 and Alex Mathie in 1995. All proved highly popular with the fans in their different ways. The gangly Marshall, described by one sports writer as looking as if he had just clambered out of a train crash, formed an effective partnership up front with the lively Mathie. The latter will be forever remembered by Town faithful for his first-half hat-trick in a 5-0 thumping of the hated Canaries on 21 February 1998 – a game which was immediately dubbed the 'Demolition Derby'.

The single blackest day in my years as an Ipswich supporter was undoubtedly 4 March 1995 when, towards the end of that relegation season, Town were hammered 9-0 by Man Utd at Old Trafford. I couldn't even escape from the humiliation abroad. Not long after, on a very cold spring day, I was in France doing a reconnaissance for a summer battlefield tour around Arras. My companion Lieutenant-Colonel Mike Martin and I were looking through the window of the Mairie in the rural village of Bullecourt when the Mayor himself - the charming Monsieur Jean Letaille – came up behind us and politely enquired about the nature of our quest. Having been invited into his nearby house and battlefield museum for a warming glass of something alcoholic, he asked where we currently lived. As soon as I said 'Ipswich', Monsieur Letaille roared with laughter and replied 'Ah! You lost 9-0 to Manchester!' Mike Martin, a lifelong Portsmouth fan, has never let me forget that moment of abject shame. He often came up for the day whenever Pompey were playing at Portman Road and, in turn, was always reminded of the afternoon when Neil Thompson blasted a last-minute free kick past the Portsmouth keeper to win the game 3-2 – so

I suppose honours are even! Mike's stentorian Army officer's voice and bubbly personality obviously left its mark on my fellow fans in the Pioneer Stand. 'How's the mad Colonel?' they would invariably enquire of me every season.

Under new manager George Burley, himself an Ipswich legend from the Robson era, and a new chairman, the urbane David Sheepshanks, there were marked and encouraging advances in the playing staff and the club's facilities from 1995 onwards. At least Sheepshanks and Burley had a 'Five-Year Plan' which gave shape, direction and co-ordination to the club's efforts on and off the field. Equally important, from my standpoint, was a noticeable return to the kind of smooth, attacking football for which Town had been rightly praised twenty years earlier. I was especially impressed by David Sheepshanks' obvious enthusiasm for the club. He was clearly a genuine fan who was known to sit sometimes among the Town supporters at away games. I liked the style of Town chairmen in general. In the days of the Cobbolds – John and Patrick – it was said that the only crisis acknowledged by the chairman and directors was when the white wine ran out in the boardroom. John Wark, in his recent autobiography, relates the story of goalkeeper Paul Cooper's home debut in August 1974. An hour before kick-off, 'Mr John' – as John Cobbold was always known – invited Paul to the boardroom for a glass of wine. When Paul pointed out that he was playing in an hour, 'Mr John' replied 'Good, you've got plenty of time!' During Town's all-too-brief renaissance in the early 2000s, David Sheepshanks was interviewed on television by Barry Davies who remarked that Ipswich was one of the few clubs where the fans in the stands actually sang the praises of the chairman. Sheepshanks explained that this was because the board, management, players and fans had a symbiotic relationship. An amused Barry Davies said that this made Town unique on *two* counts – not only did the fans like and respect the chairman, but also Sheepshanks was the first football chairman he had met who used words like 'symbiotic'!

The late 1990s were a time of growing optimism but also of recurrent and exquisite pain as, in three successive seasons, Town narrowly missed promotion by losing in the dreaded play-offs. A fresh crop of talented young players, including Richard Wright, Kieron Dyer, Titus Bramble and James Scowcroft (all Suffolk-born) blossomed before our eyes, while Burley made some clever signings to stiffen the side in crucial areas. 'Captain Fantastic' Matt Holland – a credit to the club – Jamie Clapham, Tony Mowbray, Jim 'Magic Man' Magilton, Dutchmen Fabian Wilnis and Martijn Reuser, Mark Venus, David Johnson (the second), Hermann Hreidarsson, John McGreal, Alan Armstrong and Marcus Stewart all played key roles in Town's resurgence. Some achieved cult status, such as David ('Born is the King of Portman Road') Johnson, who scored 22 goals for Town in his first season with the club, and Marcus Stewart, who netted 21 – including a hat-trick against Southampton – in Town's first season back in the Premiership. Marcus also started a fashion by wearing multi-coloured 'ITFC' gloves on the pitch from Boxing Day 2000 onwards. Yes, I'm afraid to admit, we all bought them and wore them that season!

Moreover, I finally have to confess to my friends and to the British football public at large, that – deeply passionate though I was as a fan – I actually missed two of the greatest games in Town's recent history. After the acute agony and misery of three successive play-off defeats, I had booked, in advance, a holiday in the Lakes and at the Keswick Jazz Festival for a week or so in May 2000, only to find that Town had reached the play-offs yet again and that the decisive home leg of the semi-final against Bolton would take place while I was away. With the absolutely vital life-support system of a half-bottle of scotch, I followed the game, while lying on my hotel bed, through a mixture of Ceefax and Teletext and frustratingly sporadic up-dates on a mid-week sports television programme. With Bolton leading 2-1 at half-time (i.e. with two precious away goals), and Town having missed a penalty, my fragile optimism evaporated as my language grew worse. My beloved did not help much by uttering that maddening and universal wifely mantra – 'Don't get so worked up darling, it's only twenty-two sweaty men kicking a ball!' I therefore switched the telly off for a while, feeling that ignorance would be preferable to mounting depression, before I mustered the courage to switch back on. I was overjoyed to discover that Bolton had been reduced to nine men, Ipswich were 5-3 up and – miracle of all miracles – Jim Magilton had scored a hat-trick!

Firmly convinced that my personal presence at the game might jinx the team, I chose – in a gesture of supreme self-sacrifice – *not* to apply for a ticket for the 2000 play-off final against Barnsley at Wembley. I can now reveal to the world that I could not even bear to watch it live on the television. At five to three that afternoon I went out for a long walk around the almost deserted streets of Ipswich, trying to avoid snatches of commentary which could occasionally be heard through open windows. Eventually, just as at Keswick, I plucked up the nerve to go home and cautiously opened the lounge door to find that Town were 3-2 up but hanging on with only minutes to go. Then Richard 'Bam Bam' Naylor, who had earlier come on as a substitute for the injured David Johnson and was patently having *the* game of his life, somehow prodded the ball forward while lying prone in the centre circle, putting Martijn Reuser through on goal. In a manner reminiscent of Geoff Hurst in 1966, 'Rolls' Reuser mercifully didn't try anything fancy and drove the ball high into the Barnsley net. In that wonderful moment we knew for certain that we were back in the Premiership. I spent most of the next two days endlessly playing a video recording of the game, though I did re-emerge into the sunlight to join the crowds on the Cornhill, the day after the match, to cheer the team as they appeared on the balcony of the Town Hall.

Lest I be deemed a total wimp for missing the play-off final, I must point out that I am in famous company. In 1960, Bing Crosby – co-owner of the Pittsburgh Pirates – could not bear to watch his team play the New York Yankees in the seventh and decisive game of that year's World Series, and flew to Paris to avoid jinxing them. He therefore missed seeing the Pirates triumph as Bill Mazeroski hit an electrifying home run that won the game 10-9.

For once, the following season (2000-2001) wasn't an anti-climax. Fired by Marcus Stewart's goals and bolstered by a great *team* spirit, Town incredibly finished fifth in the table and secured a place in Europe for 2001-2002. When, in our first home game, against Manchester United, Titus Bramble left Roy Keane on the floor after a fair but bone-jarring 50-50 challenge and came away with the ball, we all nodded to each other in silent agreement that 'we're going to be OK!'

A memorable day for me personally came in January 2001 when Town were away at Stamford Bridge. A comfortably-off friend of mine (we had met on a battlefield tour) put me up at his lovely Kensington home on the Friday night and, on the Saturday afternoon, we were transported to the ground in a chauffeur-driven limousine. The downside to all this was that our match seats were in the Shed End amid hostile and totally unpleasant Chelsea fans, and Town lost 4-1 after scoring first. Even so, in sixty years of watching football, I have never again arrived at a stadium in such style! It was in the 2000-2001 season too that the nickname of 'Tractor Boys' truly caught on. It appears to have been first chanted by Town fans during a game against Birmingham in 1997-1998 and was an ironic response to habitual taunts about our rural origins and derogatory chants of 'Ooh-arrr' from opposing supporters. The nickname was rapidly and widely adopted in the autumn of 2000, especially by the media, although there is evidence to suggest that George Burley and the players were none too keen on it.

The club's resurgence was great while it lasted but the revival was, in truth, desperately short. George Burley's normally sure touch in the transfer market deserted him for the 2001-2002 season. He invested unwisely in highly-paid foreign players whose wage demands apparently upset the existing, and carefully-nurtured, dressing room spirit. One such import was a flashy Italian goalkeeper, Matteo Sereni, who my late Dad would have described as 'all corduroy and blow-wave'. Another was Nigerian international Finidi George. He had a sensational home debut against Derby County, scoring twice. 'He comes from Africa and drives a big Tractor' sang the intoxicated fans. Thereafter he was largely a damp squib, making only 35 appearances and scoring seven goals in all. With the team spirit gone, Town were inevitably relegated in 2002.

Successive years of near-misses and comparative mediocrity in the Championship now ensued. Under George Burley's successor, the likeable Joe Royle, there were *some* moments of fun and optimism, as new young players such as Darren Ambrose and Darren Bent made their mark. But Royle and *his* successors as manager – Jim Magilton and Roy Keane – have since collectively failed to convince me that the halcyon days of the late 1970s and early 1980s are likely to return soon. In 2005 my wife Jane and I moved from Ipswich to Cheltenham and I regret to say that I hardly ever see the Tractor Boys live these days. The Ipswich result is *still* the first one I look for at five o'clock on a Saturday evening during the season, and I *still* feel irrationally pleased and smug when they win or downcast when they loose. However, I now see more of Cheltenham Town at Whaddon Road than Ipswich Town at Portman Road. At Cheltenham I can *stand* in the windswept 'Paddock', between the Gents and the pie stall, and can lean on the rail near the touchline. At last, after sixty-two years of going to football games, I can accuse an errant linesman of excessive and unnatural self-abuse and – given that he is only two yards away – be absolutely certain that he can hear me!! And, knowing that Cheltenham Town are not likely to win anything of significance, the pressure is off and I can enjoy each game as it comes. Yet I would probably exchange it all for just one more glimpse of John Wark stealing into the box to convert a cross from Clive Woods.

9

Liverpool

Down there for Dancing

Tony Wailey

You need not attach great importance to the rioting in
Liverpool last night. It took place in an area where disorder is
a chronic feature.
Winston Churchill, Home Secretary, June 1911.

Eddy wakes up crying and doesn't know why. Yes he does,
55 years of pain and he's only just past sixty. Reality bites
his swollen face. He still loves Mo. Supporting Liverpool
Football Club went with the pain of the separation. The
early tide outside his window rolled sullenly under a deep
purple sky. The water flecked with occasional silver. He
doesn't know where he ends and the world begins. His
condominium, the burnished windows part of the dark
refurbished brick of the Waterloo Dock part of the same
chocolate box of a changed city. A changed club, a changed
crowd, a changed team?

In *Edgy Cities*, Steve Higginson describes the city of
Liverpool as follows:

'If you follow and map the old Liverpool dock road, north to
south and back and around, the contours and outline take on an
image of a huge liner; one which is eternally docked and going
nowhere, yet still a permanent reminder of Liverpool's social shape
of time and place.

Somewhere between here and there even though the rivers edge
lies dormant, the ever present strength of the sea's rhythms still
creates differing measures of time and behaviour for those who live
within its compass. Liverpool is an Ocean town, an in between sort
of place, a place that finds itself within a temperate zone but it is
not a temperate city.'

How Eddy's old man, a Blue from a family of Blues, had
taken him to a reserve match between Liverpool and Everton,
at Anfield, a crowd of 8,000. The Old Man didn't want to but

his mother had interceded. 'Ah take him Jack if he keeps on asking'. 'It's only a reserve game' the old feller said.

Eight years old, he'd stood in front of the rusting red iron barriers on the Kop and knew that this was his place. It was a simple as that. A September afternoon in a port city over fifty years ago, his life changed forever.

Stephen Kelly in his biography of Bill Shankly points out that:

'When Shankly came five years later, standing on the brink of a new decade, the city of Liverpool could never have guessed that the sixties would rocket it to the centre of world attention. It was still an economically important city; the docks were still a thriving community. Ships would lie moored in the Mersey awaiting the next tide or a vacant birth, while the ferryboats that steamed from Liverpool to Birkenhead would meander through a maze of shipping... The whole waterfront was a whirl of ships, cranes, stevedores and chandlers. When Bill Shankly arrived ships were still an important commodity but to the discerning eye the writing was already on the wall, some docks had closed, others were half empty and the giant liners were spotted less frequently on the river. Far more depressing than the economics of the city were the fortunes of the two local football clubs. Liverpool had been trapped in the second division since 1954 and hadn't won anything since they clinched the league title in 1947, the first year after the war. Since then they had gone into steady decline. ...Everton had not fared much better. Yet Liverpool and Everton were clubs of undoubted pedigree'

He smoked a cigarette and looked at the door. The room is half in darkness. In his dream there was something about a newspaper, a newspaper full of births and deaths and Joseph O'Dea dancing in the dynamite sunshine of Buenos Aires. There was a woman. There was always a woman. A blonde woman's image appeared but he was better now and ignored another revealing of his passed life even if it went passed in the flash of a sports car..

Eddy loved the Chi-lites. Everyone in this city of a certain age and particularly from the North End docks was hard wired into Soul, Tamla Motown and Soul. He loved going down onto the docks in the early sixties, there were Cunard Yanks in shiny suits, Mods in the latest zip up jackets from New York, groups like the Searchers in every pub at lunchtime, at the Dominion, the Bramley Moore, the A1 at Lloyds, the Atlantic at Sandhills! He loved Mo. He could understand her. He thought of those old songs with a grimace. The team had risen and risen since January 1960 when Shankly took over and it wasn't until twenty five years later, half a cycle in Kondratiev's theory of econometrics that a hole was blown through that communion. Maybe if his old man had not died so soon it would have been different. He thought of those golden years and the rise of the team from winning the old second division in 1962, St John who never played in the last match losing his new suede shoes in the sea of mud as the crowd erupted onto the pitch and carried him shoulder high to the Kop. Souness leading them out at Anfield for the game against Norwich City, the draw that confirmed them as three time champions of the league in the spring of 1984, the first time for fifty years alongside Huddersfield and Arsenal.

The semi final of the FA Cup that they had never won and the longest bus ride home in history from that defeat against Leicester in 1963, He would do it a hundred times over if one Hillsborough life could have been saved; the league championship in 1964, the FA Cup a year later and then the great campaign to the semi final of the European Cup in the same year.

As the Chi Lites sang:
"You know its funny, I thought I had that woman in the palm of my hand/ it's just what I cannot understand"

Fragments: if you asked him what he remembered best apart from the all the history he would have answered fragments, bits and pieces, shadows, rain snow and sunlight. Jimmy Melia heading a last second cross into the Kop for a 2 -2 draw against Brighton two minutes after he'd missed a penalty. The place exploding with his own laughter and relief. The same Jimmy in his white shoes who brought Brighton to Anfield nearly a quarter of a century later on their way to the cup final in 1983. Billy Stevenson who came back with Stoke City, Jimmy Case with Southampton.

All of them received in thunder by the Anfield they had graced, the celebrations and tears they suffered. Terry McDermott's chip against Spurs at White Hart Lane in 1980. Michael Owen's first goal against Wimbledon at Plough Lane and his near hat trick in the last five minutes against Arsenal in the Cup Final at Cardiff when Robbie almost put him clear. The Four Seasons, The Temptations and The Marvellettes, that first season in the European Cup in 1965.

As immortalized in the arts journal *Eight Days a Week Koln 2000* which celebrated links between Liverpool and Cologne, there was snow, snow everywhere the last few days. They didn't tell you anything then, but all roads do lead to Rome. St John, writing in the paper that morning about European fans. Good supporters, but "do they know about our crowd? Bells, horns and bugles all make a noise but there is nothing like the Anfield roar."

The walking up Fountains Road and the queuing; they queued from 5 o'clock, him and the old man. He'd had a heart attack the year before so they did not go on the Kop. Twenty eight thousand heaving on the same terrace, singing and swaying and roaring under the one roof would be too much for him. So they stood in lines just by the side wall and waited for the Paddock to open. Hours later, when they opened the gates, they were still well down in the queue that stretched away to the park. The snow come down heavier in big blotched flakes and heard the roar when the Liverpool team came out in their coats to look at the pitch. When they finally stood in the ground under the floodlights you could see the wind start to drive the snow that already lay across the pitch.

They were singing over in the Kop and you wished you were in your normal space high above the goal and over towards the boys' pen. This was our first season in the European Cup but here and there you could see the flags of Anderlecht and Reykjavik where the team had been before. The ground was full before seven. There was a moan when they announced the teams. All week there had been the question on whether Rowdy Yeats would play and now the answer was no. Then the referee was out again looking at the weather, the linesmen with him, and as the snow gusted there was an army of sweepers across the pitch trying to keep the lines clear. The singing was louder now and you could see the Kop starting to sway and the steam rising up under the lights. Then the roar and the whistling as Cologne came out, all in white, white dancers on the snow and the dark heavy ball they kicked in with and the storm of noise as they ran towards the Kop.

Then the referee came out again as the Cologne players kicked about and the old man looked at his watch. It was just gone twenty past seven. The snow was driving hard now. You could see it blowing in under the Kop as if it was being sucked into a slaughterhouse, and away over you could hardly see the Anfield Road, even with the lights.

The old man kept looking at his watch. Time passed. He said, "There must be murder outside". Then we heard over the tannoy that it had been postponed. The Cologne team came onto the pitch once again and everyone thought the match was on and there was a huge roar. The Cologne players started to wave and then they went back down the tunnel and there was a lot of angry booing. Liverpool had never come out.

There was an announcement that they would all be issued 'passouts', tickets that we could use again when the match would be replayed, except in the hubbub nobody heard it on the Kop and they did not repeat it again or if they did, nobody noticed. That's when the madness started. There were nearly 50,000 in the ground and if you took away the stands that meant 43,000 passouts had to be issued. We were all right in the Paddock where there were only 5,000 tickets and a decent number of turnstiles. Even then, it took another hour of queuing. You were glad the old man had not gone on the Kop. Over there you could see the swaying and hear the angry, frustrated buzz.

You had left the house at four o'clock from the north end of the city and did not get back until nearly eleven. The snow was everywhere and all they had for seven hours out in the cold was the two swift glimmers of the Cologne team and no sight at all of the beloved Reds. The Old Man was a Blue but he loved the European games. You followed the team home and away until you went to sea and knew you would not make the following game as the ship was leaving in a few days' time to go 'around the land', before the sugar run to the West Indies. On the way home as the bus crawled and the snow drove through the streets of. Bootle and Seaforth and Waterloo, you looked at the yellow ticket then passed it over to the old feller.

At the dock, catering superintendents would be waiting anxiously, half tide lock gate men with bicycle clips around their ankles, deck superintendents, customs officials, shore gangs, hangers on, shift watchmen, all wanting us away so they could get onto their next ship. Shouting and trying to jump aboard for smokes as a ship came home. Now you were costing them money by staying. The ship would go out through the great churning locks, the blackened wood of the inner gates of the Canada basin. And never a night when there would not be a Dockers gang to be working under the lights, coats folded against the winter weather, the sweet smells of their tobacco filling the bus home after the football. Smells that you had grown up with. Stuff that couldn't be changed, but you wouldn't see that game again.

All he remembers was the snow and the singing and the white shirts of Cologne and the navy blue pull up collar of the goalkeeper. That guy played his heart out two weeks later as you stayed glued to the ship's radio then went ashore in Glasgow. Poor, sweet, devastated Glasgow where you were bought drinks and shook our heads as we watched the television highlights of 'Toni' Schumacher making his wonderful saves. The old man went again and took one of the cousins with him on the strength of that yellow ticket.

So much was happening that season, not only with the European Cup but also with the FA Cup run which we had never won in our entire history. There were replays and overlapping games every week. Three days after the Cologne postponement we played Leicester away and drew in the sixth round, then played them in a replay the following Wednesday, then a league match on the Saturday, then the Cologne game again, then another league game, then the third Cologne game, then the semi-final of the Cup three days later. 'We all went down to Villa Park, Haroo Haroo' was one of the songs. Apart from one league game, we won everything. This was the season that we started to understand what playing in Europe really meant.

The lesson extended to the San Siro where Liverpool lost to more than just two controversial goals, the bribing and later suspension of the Spanish referee and Yugoslavian linesman. We lost some more of our naiveté' too. We learnt an awful lot from Europe that season but none more so than from Cologne. They showed us that to draw away was not always good enough in this company. Some of our greatest triumphs have echoed this truth. Three decades later it is only Madrid that matches our nine consecutive seasons in the 'real' champion's league.

It was funny really that one of the ship's boilers developed a fault and, instead of a straight passage from Liverpool to Barbados, the Harrison boat had to put into San Nazaire, the port for Nantes on the west coast of France, where we had our first game in Europe in the Anglo Italian Cup or in some other Mickey Mouse competition around the turn of the Sixties, 1960 maybe. You got murder at home staying behind for autographs and coming back on the last bus because the French players had stayed behind for a drink. It was from there, with the evening light sweeping the quayside, and the sky across the Atlantic, with packets of yellow cigarettes, drinks of Pernod and a mountain of small beers before you, that we again saw the highlights, flickering from a television in the Dockers' bar.

You saw Rowdy Yates toss the coin, and St John hold his head in his hands. We thought he'd lost it, then they tossed again after the coin got stuck in the mud and St John was dancing up and down and being joined by Billy Stevenson and Rowdy himself. Three Scotsmen all dancing in Springtime Rotterdam.

Someone wrote later "that Cologne should go down after 300 minutes' play and after a great rally tonight was a subject almost for tears". We did not shed any but we knew there had been a fight and we knew the matches would be remembered as a classic. They still do in Cologne.

That song by The Beautiful South comes to mind, "Everywhere is Rotterdam and everywhere you roam. Everywhere is Rotterdam in Liverpool or Rome". It might have been coined for us that night except you were cheated by Inter Milan who knew very well that the final would be at their home ground, the San Siro in May that year.

Later, while we sat sweating in the Hurricane ports, the old man sent a letter. He said simply, "That goalie, for a fat man, made some saves. He must have been wearing the shamrock". It all seemed a long way from the soldiers clearing the railway lines and the roads across Merseyside that early March night in 1965. The snow blotching everywhere, the queues and the singing rising up into the air and the long walk down Fountains Road with the smells of the ale houses and the chip shops and the black mass of the docks below you and the lights on the river where the Harrison boats docked.

The letter was for later. It wasn't snow that blew around you but the dynamite heat and humidity as they sat at anchor and listened to the BBC's World Service for commentary of the European Cup final. Inter Milan might have cheated us, Cologne might have fought us to the toss, but it was the Reds who should have been there at the final that year. We would be back.

Eddy was a Tamla Motown boy and it was where his company derived its name but he wouldn't forget the injustice. He loved the Temptations and Smoky Robinson but it was the Chi Lites who sang his song. It wouldn't leave his head. It wasn't like the great Miracles singing:

'If I appear carefree, it's only to counter last night's sadness'

No it was more than that, the Chi Lites burnt into his soul as much as the earlier copperplate hand of his old man and his letters.

'I hear her voice as the cold winds blow/ or on the sweet music of the radio'

Eddy knew he had messed up. Had fucked up as badly as a shooting star screams its brilliant passage then falls out of the night sky onto the white sand of some lonely atoll. But forgiveness was within her, it was why he loved her. It wasn't physical any more but he loved the way she held herself, her silks and linens in summer, her red woollen jackets in winter as if she hadn't a care. As though she knew everything would be all right, the way she walked in all weather. She held the world in her hand when she looked at him, if that was what you called love. When she met him for a coffee in town. When she drank slowly, eyes above the cup, looking away suddenly. Forgiveness does that for you. He didn't know if it had worked for his sons.

He remembered going down to see Christy. He sat down and looked around the place; the brown and yellow walls, the red and blue plastic chairs in the lobby. It was when he sat and looked he got scared. He shivered inside himself. He knew that as soon as he had arrived, thought it was different from the old days, just breeze in, jump from dock to dock, sign on and laugh around with his son but time had come in the way between them.

He missed the rhythms of the jazz musician Gerry Mulligan at lunch times, around the house, say, or looking at the light over the garden, the railway and the fields. He missed that cool and fluent Mulligan sound, the deep sax flowing out, and Miles Davis following up, the beat weaving around him, through his still-tired eyes, through his resting brain. His family asleep upstairs, yeah, he missed those days, the ease and warmth he felt when he thought about his home. The home he had broken twice. Now his sons in doss houses all across the city. Great Stuff, he'd been a real success. His warm home long gone.

'I'm used to having someone to lean on and I'm lost, Baby I'm lost'

He couldn't blame the football but it was all part of the same process. You didn't think it could have all come to this. So confident, so confident and that confidence took us through the golden age of the next twenty years. And even when the city was being hammered from the late 1970s and the 1980s, the Reds kept on winning. And winning well. And because Everton were going through the Gordon Lee years the team became a beacon for a whole City's resistance until Everton became great again in the middle 'Eighties. Only Aston Villa and Arsenal, by the slimmest margin in the history of the football league, stopped Merseyside, Liverpool (7) and Everton (2) from winning every league championships between 1980 and 1990. This was at the same time as when the whole of the industrial infrastructure, built so delicately after the war, was being torn apart and the city bled thousands of Jobs and thousands more of its population. When his old man was growing up there was nearly a million people here. It was half that by the end of the century. 'The City of a horrifying example' as one newspaper put it.

You didn't have to know anything about loss to know that Heysel and Hillsborough blew a hole through the soul of the club. One would have been a disaster for any club or team or City to deal with, to experience them both within the space of four years was a nightmare.

He had always been Labour because of the family and because of the ships and the North End docks but in the wider city, Liverpool only became Labour in the 1960s when the protestant working class stopped voting Conservative, in Walton, Kirkdale, on the Dingle. Labour was where the young and the city were heading in the cultural revolution of that decade but even if Everton and Liverpool were two very conservative clubs the mass singing didn't surprise anyone. It was part of a forward march of the time, now all of it had seemed to come to a halt, but it mattered in terms of resistance.

If Everton were supposed to be the Catholic team and Liverpool the Protestant, that was all done and dusted by the end of the Second War. It meant that even if you are talking about Liverpool Football Club you couldn't talk just of them in a city like Liverpool. There is too much history, too much intertwining, too much family from Everton who are still the fourth most successful team in the premier division. They also suffered in those terrible years of the 'Eighties and the terrible irony was when they found a way back with a wonderful young team, the awful tragedy of Heysel blocked their progression into the European Cup. Much of the bitterness that has built up between supporters stems from this date but there was nothing of religion about it and neither was it cultural. It was born out of resistance and frustration.

A quarter of a century later Eddy wrote to the local paper – about relationships between the Blue and the Red. He remembered the sack of letters that come before the twenty-fifth anniversary of the first great tragedy. Tormented by Heysel and the terrible loss of life, the club apologised on behalf of and with its supporters in April 2005 when Juventus came to Anfield in the European Champions League. Despite the provocation, and there was terrible provocation including the stabbings at the European Cup final the year before in 1984, Eddy recognised that they were still our supporters. 'Ours,' despite the fact that the greatest club Secretary, Peter Robinson, had publicly condemned UEFA's decision months before the game for the staging of the fixture at the *decrepit state of the stadium* and, most importantly, the ticketing arrangements. But those fans were still 'Ours'. He remembered those sad silent trains coming back to Liverpool on the Friday morning, the vast majority of the supporters gutted and forlorn. We had lost our great name in Europe. In his letter published in the *Liverpool Daily Post* on the 9th October 2008, he said;

'As a "mad" Red of a certain age, I read with sympathy Ron Noon's letter (October 3) where he spoke of the great work done by Liverpool Unites being undone by young Evertonians chanting "murderers" at Liverpool fans and invoking once again, after nearly a quarter of a century, the tragic events of the Heysel Stadium.

Ron comments that: "After Heysel, and coming up to the 20th anniversary of Hillsborough, a time when all Scousers, Blue or Red were united in grief, no decent fans ought ever to hear such calumny.

Like thousands of others, we started in the Boys Pen in the late 1950s and gradually moved up to the back (Cell Block H as Roy Evans described it) and closer to the Kop as we grew older and, like Ron, have family who are split down the middle in football persuasion.

My Old Man was an ardent Blue but who loved his European football, and had his second heart "murmur" after being in the paddock for the Cologne game (postponed) in 1965. My son is an equally passionate Evertonian, who welcomed Liverpool FC home in 2005. These events 40 years apart are important, two passionate Blues going to witness "European events" that took them outside the boundaries of their team, but not of their own city.

These two events are also important in terms of dates, for they divide Heysel, and it is precisely that loss of "Europeanness" that Evertonians feel most deprived.

That at one crucial moment of their history, when they had a great team, were league champions had just won the European Cup Winners' Cup and were, some would argue, about to reach their great moment in Europe, the events at Heysel unfolded and deprived them of everything with the banning of the English clubs after that disaster.

I have often felt, and am not alone, that Liverpool supporters have not apologised enough for those events of 1985.

Too much was going on in that decade in the city, too many tragedies, too many setbacks, too many things to face as the city looked as if it was closing down.

But on public displays during that time, the Blue half of the city always showed its support, just as the city has come together for Liverpool Unites and the murder of the young Blue, Rhys Jones, last year.

Can I just offer then, a deep and heartfelt apology to all our Blue friends for what was denied them – a sense of their European dream, in which we as Reds take such pride.

If sorry is such a little word, then there, I've said it again.

Please forgive us and let's see if we can move on.'

There'd been a number of women since his wife left him but the red brick shine of the evening on the corner of Ullett Road, the Doll's House, that cool and fluent Mulligan sax, never let him go. He was richer there in his own home with his wife when he compared it to this box. He felt best where he had once been. It took him years to admit that and not drink himself stupid.

He wore good clothes. They got better as the business improved. Dove grey suits or a blue Worsted, pin stripe if he was going to the bank in town, mohair on the docks. His shoes were always brown or cherry red. It reminded him of his Motown days and his Comos and Camel coat. Who cared what his face was like? The bruises and cut across the top of the nose would wait. He knew he had to take that contract. He was talking to his son, the son that raised his fists to him. "Someone else has to ring the bell now," he said.

He was no longer looking at the dull gold of his wedding ring. The small but expensive chains across his shoes. The choker that shone against his neck when Mo first presented it to him in their bedroom. Their house that he and she had worked so hard to keep, all shining brasses and white plaster and a little picket fences when she had forced him from Maghull and back to the streets they called the Dales. How was he to understand the measure of the nightmares, the burning in between worlds, the old man's generous heart, the eldest son's fists, the city's fight to get back on terms in the latter 1980s and then the next disaster and the utter betrayal in the wake of its aftermath in 1989.

Nothing can describe Hillsborough. Not at the time and not now. But if ever there was a moment when the club became emblematic of the city's soul it was then, when it threw open its doors to anyone and everyone. The Kop became a meditative, cavernous chapel, every crush barrier a votive offering, the pitch a shrine and moving sea of flowers. It was there that the club became a rock – a meeting place for fans, for its community, for bereft families and for children. You have to look no further than one of the great heroes of that moment, Kenny Dalglish, who conducted himself beyond what was expected of any footballer or football manager and came to symbolise the spirit of the city.

Forget that he was the greatest player to pull on the red shirt. He could have been Shankly's son to understand that spirit, that affinity with the people with his great compassion and unwavering face. Head bowed through all the sad funerals when some of the players, who'd also given everything, couldn't take any more. And yet if you read his memoirs, *My Liverpool Home*, Kenny talks of Hillsborough nearly breaking him both physically and mentally. This was the same across the whole city. Eddy would never forget the Evertonions who stood shoulder to shoulder with everything, especially with the boycott of the Sun newspaper and its lies, who whistled at the National Anthem at Wembley and sang, 'Merseyside, Merseyside' in 1989; despite the six apologies, a boycott which still continues to this day through the *Justice for the Ninety Six* campaign.

Eddy would vote for Andy Burnham in the Labour Leadership election for having the guts to come to Anfield on the 20th Anniversary of Hillsborough in 2009 and stand there silent, grim faced while 28,000 roared for such justice, for questions still to be answered, for an apology to be given. Eddy would vote for him for his message of taking this feeling back to a Labour Government, for the files to be opened and not be subject to a thirty year censorship. For a terrible symmetry of heartbreak and tragedy to be eased, for so many burdens still to be carried in this least English of English cities.

But if you mentioned Kenny you also needed a word here for Rafael Benitez, that most stubborn of men and the worst of listeners but who also understood very well what Hillsborough meant to the city. Despite all the strictures and importunities he took the Club to the verge of three European Champions League Finals between 2005 and 2008 and recovered its European Cup identity. A man who along with his assistant Paco Ayestaran knew what the club meant in the soul of its fans.

In his detailed account, *A Season on the Brink: Rafa Benitez, Liverpool and the Path to European Glory*, Guillem Balague points out:

Ayesteran, a big fan of photography was also determined that Melwood, the training ground's historic aura should not be lost.' I asked for three photos of the Liverpool supporters to be hung up at Melwood he explains,' one had to be with the fans celebrating something like a goal. Another with them suffering, because they do suffer; they go home and they don't sleep and it is not the same getting up the next day....finally I wanted a photo just showing them supporting the team. Now these shots are on the wall and look down on us each morning. The players need to respect these people and think about those types of situations. Liverpool players should never forget that as footballers they have a privileged and important role.

Eddy knew the tragedy for Benitez was that he lost or fell out with Ayesteran and the manager was never the same again given his penchant for the myopic and sometimes arrogant way he decided the team should play. The failure of the players he bought after Paco's departure. The gains of the great season of 2008-2009 when the club finished runners up, its best performance in the league for 19 years were left to wither away. The tragedy was that after two years, Rafa's tenure became inextricably involved in the same process as the civil war over the ownership issue that was eating the club alive.

There were those who did well out of the de-industrialisation of Britain in the 1980s with the defeats of the Miners and Dockers and Seamen, the closure of the factories and the dwindling in the production of Steel. The likes of security firms like Group 4 and the transport companies like TNT all boomed when the State fell away. But they were like pilot fish to the real winners of that decade; Rupert Murdoch's empire and his move from newsprint to computer and to terrestrial broadcasting after the battering of the print unions and the demise of Fleet Street at a disused dock in Wapping.

This not only left its own legacy but bound itself up with, not entirely co-incidentally, the development of the Premier League. The huge amounts of money pushed into the League by Sky Television created a totally different relationship between clubs and fans; crucially the relationship between club and owners and financial capital. Murdoch was a symbol of what the urban geographer Manuel Castells terms *info capitalists.*

Someone once commented that whilst Manchester United started to operate at this time of the Premier League as if they were running a superstore, Liverpool in the sixteen years that David Moores (1991-2007) took over as chairman was still being run like a Co-operative corner shop.

They also had the good luck of being able to develop their ground upwards, adding new tiers like at Barcelona but something not possible for Liverpool – hemmed in by the tight terraced community of Anfield. Every football supporter knows, despite the adroitness of management and ultimate buying of success at Chelsea, obtaining another ground does not even enter into their calculations but Liverpool were stuck. A club that had always tailored their ticket prices to the knowledge that it was a poor city were left with little other options. Even today buying a season ticket at Liverpool is akin to putting your new born child down for Eton just as in the 1960s and 1970s, Liverpool attendances were always higher than those of Manchester United: not any more.

When the Scouser and Old Etonian David Moores wanted to sell the club it was into this boiling vat that he was dipping his toes. Not content to sell to an established dynasty from the Arabian peninsula with a Liverpool supporting executive, he and his chief executive Rick Parry instead plumped for the leveraged, geared up, factored in, bought out structures of guess games and smoke and mirrors which George Gillett and Tom Hicks were infamously responsible for in the United States.

As the *Daily Mail* on the 7th February 2007 reported:

'Parry admitted that Hicks' involvement was crucial in swaying the decision in Gillett's favour after he had originally lost out to the Dubai investors. Hicks said the Premiership's new TV deal had persuaded him to join the bid when he and Gillett formulated their plan last week.'

Gillett added: "This is a tribal sport like nothing we've seen in America."

He pointed out that, unlike Glazer's takeover of Old Trafford, the club had been saddled with no debt'

For Parry to collaborate with this deliberate economy of truth and state that when the leverage genius came in to partner George Gillett in March 2007 'it made the bid that much more compelling' will go down as one of the most inane statements ever made by any senior officer of Liverpool Football club, let alone its chief executive.

The last time Liverpool experimented with a power share, Roy Evans and Gerard Houllier sat side by side and talked about a bright future. We all know what happened then'

The trail of destruction is there for all to see since 2007. That the club was sold within a fit of pique and without due diligence - Moores felt he was being 'pressurised' by the DIC Dubai Company who had completed all the necessary paperwork over six weeks, and instead 'gave it over on a word' from the Americans - that the Rothschild bank vouched for them only adds to both the irony and the tragedy.

Since then we have had bankers' requisitions, high court orders, more leveraged bidders, counter bids and prevention of bids, the pontificators of the FA, unctuous as ever and washing their hands. (Bring back the existential Graham Kelly.) And where does it leave us? The game was once local and now it is global, but what's changed? As far back as 1984, Peter Robinson reckoned 50 per cent of Liverpool's support came from outside the city. Club ownership has followed the trajectory of the Murdoch model of info capitalism but without the savvy. You don't need to be a Marxist to know that as Karl Marx argued in *The Communist Manifesto* '...capital chases the bourgeoisie across the face of the earth.' The outcome; a club, to this date, the most successful in British Football may soon enter into 'receivership'

'I hear her voice as the cold winds blow/ or on the sweet music of the radio'

Eddy thought, "I miss you Mo, I miss you" and almost laughed.

Yet here he was catching sight of mates he used to go to the match with years before. They are waving him up with them onto the plateau of St George's Hall. The latest mass demonstration called on the fourth of July to protest against the iniquities of the American Owners. Independence; Yes that's what we want, independence from these shysters.

Organised by the 10,000 strong *Spirit of Shankly – Liverpool Supporters Union*, John Aldridge is up there on the stage and John Power from the La's and Pete Wylie from the Mighty Wah is banging out, 'Heart as big as Liverpool' and Eddy knows why he has come and Howie Gayle, another local boy and hero of the Bayern Semi Final in Munich nearly 30 years ago is urging:

'Give us back our club, Mister, Give us back our club'

And Eddy knows why he's here and looks around him and see the veterans of all those long Liverpool Campaigns, The O'Neils, The Duffys, The Maguires, the spirits of Lenny Campbell and the Scottie Roader, Bobby Wilcox who spent their days and nights on the starlit roads of Europe. The talk is of bogus companies and rogue holdings, the scams the Americans had perpetrated in our name, who was taking what and loading the debt onto the club, the Cayman Island investment trust loaning money then charging high interest to the Club, already owned by the owners themselves. The RBS, the taxpayers' bank who had already received £100 million in interest payments out of the club. The speaker leaned face forward into the crowd, a man whose voice came off the lower deck.

'Our financial arm will be called Spirit of Shankly, Liverpool Credit Union. This is about creating a lasting legacy for future generations of our support, a chance for the club to be run by passionate fans not leveraged buy out merchants. We want our say and whether it is a 100% or a smaller stake in the club, we intend to have it.'

Someone turns to Eddy and says:

"How d'yuh think all these supermarkets and the land around the docks is being bought and transformed? The start of it all is through the dust. The housing schemes, the leisure complexes, the new stadium. And you know what the best is?"

Drunk. His head bobbing as he shifted from foot to foot.

"The club is only a front for their other stuff"

"You know all this don't you?"

Eddy turned his hands over, palms up, the way the old world suddenly becomes new for anyone staring into the void. He was a Liverpool supporter. He remembered the away trips to Bristol Rovers and Plymouth Argyle. The great point secured at Leyton Orient in 1962, the runners up that made sure we knew we would go up and go up as champions. Security. Fifty years later he made money by knowing things. That's why he wore a suit and went home early. The image of the blonde woman in a green sports car coming out of the car park beneath Tsao's the Chinese restaurant rose up before him.

Coming out of the Holiday Inn, anyone could have noticed the change to her hair, to her car to her black tee shirt and designer pink scarf. His ex wife was keeping one step ahead. That was all. The balance of both worlds, like Uncle Joe had gone to Argentina on a Pacific steam Navigation boat and lost the woman who loved him. Despite the divorces, the broken promises, his broken agreements – the life had been a good one, the club ran through his soul. Sometimes he wished it wasn't this way, the turning over the television when the match came on, the empty silences in the house when they lost. The reason why he wakes up crying, fifty-five years later; the celebrations that seemed such a long time ago. Jesus, he was just gone Sixty but wouldn't see Seventy at this rate.

Shankly's granddaughter was up on the steps now; she's travelled all the way from Greece, arms outstretched for the photographers. They are trying to get her to pose like her grand dad but it was more the way David Fairclough held his arms out after scoring against Saint Etienne or the ghost goal of Luis Garcia, nicked against Chelsea twenty eight years later, when Anfield rocked as it had never rocked and so defeated José Mourinho it left him scarred. And she's saying how proud her grandfather would have been of them, '...greater than the support given to Chairman Mao' standing there on these very steps in 1971 when Liverpool had been beaten in the final by Arsenal. Eddy remembered her Nana, Nessie, being led across the field to the Kop, hand in hand with Joe Fagan and Mrs Paisley, their shadows in front of them, at the last ever game in 1994 after which you could no longer stand on that terrace or lean yourself into a comfortable position in front of the red barriers...

'Who remembers Jeremy Goss?'

That we would rise again like Epstein's nude sailor outside Lewis's made him laugh. Rise again, God knows what will happen but the fans are everything with their songs and flags and banners. Liverpool football club has always shown its best side to Europe. This is still an Ocean town.

As Steve Higginson argued in *Edgy Cities*:

When Luis Borges, John Lennon, Marlon Brando, Caravaggio and Albert Camus defined their port cities there was always something of the in between time about them. These were writers who operated from the melting pot, in between hybrid places and they weren't always particular about their definition of political terms but justice always figured in there somewhere.

And Istanbul 2005 in another port city really was a miracle, where the different generations of Liverpool's supporters, blown here and there by the trade winds of fortune, were re-united with their history. *'Rafa is the Boss for us'* read one of the banners. Richard Williams' article the next day on the 26th May, in the *The Guardian* newspaper, stated, 'Like I say, it takes imagination.' He could say that again. We would need every bit of it in the coming months.

'She left her kiss upon my lips and left her print upon my heart'

Eddy didn't need any reference. Instead he thought of waking up this morning, his first cigarette, staring like a dog fox at the door and feeling like crying, loving his wife who had gone from him, just as the league championship was missing these last two decades. He was thinking of lying in the arms of a young woman and missing his old man. Who thinks stuff like that? What fool would exchange a life for your football team? Time on the Plateau, – like the anthem *Poor Scouser Tommy*, Liverpool Football Club ran through his soul.

He was not alone.

10

Port Vale

Who Would a Valiant Be

John M. Bourne

We've all arrived there countless times. Sometimes in developing relationships; more often in casual conversations. The point of declaration. 'So who do you support then?' For some reason one of these occasions has lodged itself in my mind. It was a balmy Saturday in May 1996. I was on a train to Birmingham from York, where I had been lecturing. A group of lads got into my carriage at Leeds. I don't know what they had been doing there (other than drinking). The football season was over and they were Sheffield Wednesday fans bound for a night's clubbing in Sheffield. At one point their conversation turned to the experience of being a travelling football fan, especially the places they least liked visiting. 'Stoke,' said one of them, 'that's a real sh*thole.' I was born in the Potteries (aka 'the City of Stoke-on-Trent'). All my family come from there. Although I haven't lived in the Potteries since I was eighteen, there is a sense in which I have never left it. As soon as I arrived at university I realised that there was a hard core of people in the outside world who, unaccountably, thought the Potteries was ugly, whereas we natives know that it has the beauty of Venice, the sophistication of New York and the welcoming warmth of Dublin. I could not let this insult go unanswered. 'Oi, you,' I said, 'wash your mouth out, you're talking about my home town.' (I must pause here for a little clarification. My home town is actually Burslem, one of the six that make up the City of Stoke-on-Trent. Although I love the Potteries, I hate 'Stoke-on-Trent', a fabricated abomination whose centenary we are currently 'celebrating'. During 'dead time', in dentists' waiting rooms or on station platforms, I sometimes find myself devising exquisite tortures for everyone concerned with the governance of the city, especially its wretched planners. Sorry, but I had to get that off my chest. Back to the story.) 'Are you a Stoke fan, then?' came the reply. The first insult was bad enough, but this was beyond the pale. I gave them my best glare, the one I like to describe as 'my Clint Eastwood'. I cannot summon this milk-curdling look at will. I have to be seriously annoyed. Then, in the measured tones of Dirty Harry, I spoke. 'I would rather immerse my head in a bucket of warm vomit than support Stoke City,' I said. This induced a moment of thoughtfulness among the group, but I knew what was coming next. 'Who do you support then?' 'Port Vale is my team,' I said.

My declaration was followed by another silence. I am used to this. People don't have a set response where Port Vale is concerned. One of the lads assumed a worried look that could be read as 'this bloke seems harmless but he may be a nutter, better be careful'. This is not unusual. But some response from them was clearly called for. I was ready for any of the common ones. Cutting edge wits eventually manage 'well, someone has to, I suppose'. I usually greet this with a wan smile, just sufficient to acknowledge that the spirit of Oscar Wilde lives on. Another common response is 'that's in Wales, isn't it?' I never quite know what to do about this ludicrous question that does not involve a serious assault on the enquirer's intelligence and education or an actual act of physical violence. I suppose they think Port Vale is the bastard offspring of a one-night stand between Port Talbot and Ebbw Vale. But what I got on this occasion was 'why do you support them then?' This is the perfect starting point for my football odyssey.

I gave the lads my standard answer. 'Because the first captain of Port Vale, Enoch Hood, lived next door to my grandmother.' This is not strictly true. He didn't. But he lived not far away. It is simply a neat way of expressing that Port Vale has been a part of my family's world ever since the club came into existence. The question 'why do you support them then?' implies that I had a choice, a consumer's choice, that at some point I ordered a copy of *Which Football Club?* and decided that Port Vale had what I was looking for. There are people who choose football clubs on this basis, the main criteria for choosing them being that they are famous, glamorous and win things. It's a free country. They can do what they like. And I am free to despise them. I did not choose to become a Port Vale fan. I was born one.

(A digression. It was not quite so clear that my sons were cradle Valiants. Both were born in Birmingham. My wife is from Bolton, but – thankfully – she hates football, so there was no conflict of loyalties between mum and dad. Both sons showed an early interest in the game. I took Peter to his first match when he was nearly seven, a nil nil draw against Northampton Town on 3 May 1986. This was our last home game of the 1985-86 season. We had already secured promotion to Division 3 and at the end of the game the crowd (including me and Peter) invaded the pitch, easier said than done at Vale Park in those days. This was the first time I had ever set foot on the hallowed turf – it was surprisingly bumpy. 'Crikey,' I thought, 'I hope Peter doesn't think all games end like this.' It was destined to be the last home game we played in the lowest tier of English senior football for twenty-two years. I took Tom to his first game when he was five. It was against Mansfield Town on 18 April 1987. We were losing two nil with thirteen minutes to go when moody winger Paul Smith began to run riot. The final score was Vale 3 Mansfield 2. 'Crikey,' I thought, 'I hope Tom doesn't think all games end like this.' He was destined not to see Vale lose for another twenty-two games and that in an FA Cup tie against Manchester City. Shortly after Tom's Vale baptism, I took the boys to one side. 'Look,' I said, 'daddy has something important to say. Daddy is a liberal. I won't be upset if you are not interested in football and don't want to go to matches. But if you do, you have to support the Vale. Got it?' They nodded solemnly, opted to go to matches and kept their word.)

I have unusual powers of recall. I can remember my sister being born, three days after my own third birthday. I have very clear memories of my formidable maternal grandmother, who died a month after my sister was born. But, try as I might,

I can locate no football related memories until I was nearly five. This memory is indelible. Saturday, 27 March 1954. The 1953-54 season was a special one, perhaps the most special in Vale history. The team won the Third Division (North) by eleven points, losing only three games (all of them away from home), scoring 74 goals and conceding only 21, a record for a 46-game season that stood until 1996, when it was broken by Gillingham, an achievement for which I have yet to forgive the Gills. The miserly five goals that the Vale conceded at home, however, is a record that still stands. No wonder they were known as the 'Iron Curtain' team. On top of this the Vale had a spectacular FA Cup run that saw them defeat cup holders, Blackpool, Stan Matthews and all, in the Fifth Round. When my father died I found among his papers a copy of the *Staffordshire Weekly Sentinel*, a broadsheet whose front page was covered in photographs of 'the play and the crowds' of this game. I am looking at it, framed, on the wall of my study as I write. The run ended in the semi-final against West Bromwich Albion at Villa Park, never a lucky ground for the Vale. The Baggies were going for a cup and league double. They did win the cup, denying Tom Finney a winners' medal, but came second in the league to Wolves. The Vale scored first through Albert Leake, but the Baggies won with two second-half goals from former Vale player Ronnie Allen, the second a disputed penalty. The first I knew of any of this was when my dad returned from the game. My mother and I heard the gate and rushed to the door before dad could knock. I remember the brush of her skirt as I pushed past her to get to the door. I can see my dad now. He was wearing an overcoat with a large black and white rosette on the left side. He was not wearing a hat. He usually wore a beret, known as a 'tam', being a great believer that a warm head and dry feet kept you free of all known illnesses, which in his case they largely did. I presume the supporters' coach had stopped off somewhere en route from Birmingham. It was very dark outside and the air was cold enough to taste. My dad looked drained. I am convinced there were tears in his eyes. He said two words, 'bloody robbed', and stepped past us into the bosom of his home.

Looking back, I think the 1954 semi-final defeat took something out of my dad that he never got back. If I were being fanciful I would say that it robbed him of hope, hope that little clubs could ever get a fair crack of the whip (or the little man for that matter). Or perhaps, it was just energy and enthusiasm he lost. He was already forty-five in 1954. As he trudged steadily towards his fifties, a time when he was working shifts, including nights, his attendance at matches waned. On the few occasions he took me to games I felt that he was performing a fatherly duty, taking me because I wanted to go, not because he wanted to go. But the FA Cup could still engage him. He went to the Fifth Round tie at home to Aston Villa in February 1960, a game that saw Vale's biggest ever crowd, 49,768, one club record that will never be beaten. I spent the afternoon with my friend Peter Clarke trying to guess the ebb and flow of the game by the roars of the crowd, discernible even in our street, a mile away. Villa won 2-1.

My dad's last hurrah as a spectator was probably the epic Fourth Round FA Cup replay against Sunderland on 31 January 1962. We had drawn at Roker Park, nil nil, the previous Saturday. There was a crowd of over 28,000, the biggest I had ever been in at that time. This was the era of terracing and unsegregated crowds. We stood in the Railway Paddock. I remember the crowd being very adult and male and the smell of pipe smoke. My Auntie Maud gave me some treacle toffee for the match. The press of bodies was so close that I could not get my hands into my pockets during the game. The heat generated succeeded in melting the toffee into one block that stuck to the inside of my trousers. When I finally managed to extract it, well after the end of the game, it looked like something that would not have been out of place in the ruins of Pompeii. This was the first really big occasion game I had been to. It did not disappoint. The Vale goalie, Ken Hancock, suffered an ankle injury very early on. There were no substitutes in those days, so Hancock, a fine player, had to soldier on, hopping about on one leg. This seemed to inspire the team and especially the two wingers, Brian Jackson, on the right, and the awesome

Colin Grainger, on the left. I regard Grainger as one of the unfulfilled talents of English football. He won the first of his seven England caps (as a Sheffield United player) in a 4-2 win over Brazil at Wembley in May 1956. Grainger scored twice, the first one with his first touch of the ball. (Tommy Taylor scored the other two and England missed two penalties!) Grainger was the only authentic genius I have ever seen in a Port Vale shirt. He tortured Sunderland that night. You could see panic in their players' faces every time he got the ball. On one occasion in the second-half he dropped his shoulder and sent the entire Sunderland back four the wrong way. I have only seen two other players do this: Stanley Matthews and George Best. The Vale won 3-1, with goals from Jackson, Harry Poole and Arthur Longbottom. I can remember nothing about the second and third goals, but I can still see Jackson's, a drive from the edge of the box at the Hamil Road end. I was right in line with him when he hit it. The following day the *Daily Herald* headline read 'Sunderland Cup Hopes Sink in Port', which made a change from all the 'Vale of Hope/Triumph/Despair/ Tears/Woe' headlines we've had to put up with over the years. This game also has an honoured place in my memory because of something my dad did. There was a loud Sunderland fan near us. He was well fuelled for the occasion. As the game ran away from Sunderland he began to eff and blind. My dad said quietly to him 'mind your language, there's children around' (i.e. me). And the man did. I had never thought of my dad as much of an authority figure. He was essentially a kind, sentimental man, but he had a 'work face' as well as a 'family face'. He was one of nature's NCOs. When he spoke men did as they were told. In later years an old school friend, Harry Lawton, had a student summer job working alongside my dad. We met one day in the pub after work. 'Eh,' said Harry, 'I always thought your dad was an amiable, easy going bloke, but at work he's dead scary.'

Lots of football fans are sustained through the lean years (and most years are lean years for most fans) by the Legend of the Golden Age. During the Long Dark Night of Leeds

United dominance under Don Revie, Huddersfield Town fans dreamed of Herbert Chapman's teams and prayed that they would come again, like King Arthur back to Camelot. Even fans of mighty Manchester United were forced to draw on reserves of hope accumulated under Sir Matt Busby for a generation between the European Cup win of 1968 and the Championship victory of 1993. For Port Vale fans of my generation, it was the Legend of '54. A few years ago I asked the Vale goalkeeper of that era, Ray King, to sign a copy of his autobiography, *Hands, Feet & Balls*. I mentioned that although I had never seen the 1954 team play I could still recite their names. 'Go on then,' he said. 'King; Turner; Cheadle; Sproson; Potts; Askey: Mullard; Griffiths; Cunliffe; Hayward; Leake,' I said without drawing breath. King gave me a steely look and held out his hand. 'Shake, son,' he said. Vale's stay in the old Division 2 lasted three seasons. The great team of '54 was not reinforced and gradually began to fall apart and they were relegated in 1957. The first time I remember crying over football was when I learned of the 7-1 home defeat that season by Nottingham Forest, for whom Eddie Bailey scored a hat-trick. Bailey has the honour of being the first of my Totally Irrational Hatreds in Football. I am sure that he was a very decent man and a very fine player, but I still remember him principally for the pain he inflicted on me that day. I know I should have got over it by now, but I haven't. Nottingham Forest is also high on my list of Clubs I Have Never Seen the Vale Beat But Would Really Like To. The journey back to Camelot was to prove long and bumpy and, often, seemingly impossible.

Philip Larkin famously described his childhood as a 'forgotten boredom'. Mine, in memory at least, was a kind of magical mystery tour. I can recall whole episodes with total clarity; other parts are a complete blank. But even when I can remember what happened it is often difficult to work out why. My first visit to Vale Park to see the first team play is a typical example. My dad didn't take me. I didn't go with friends. My friend Peter Clarke's dad, Percy (a lovely man), took me. Just me and him. This was not planned. I was standing by our gate.

I can see Mr Clarke walking down the street now. As he got to me, he said 'I'm going up the Vale, do you want to come?' I did not need to be asked twice. Nor did I think there was anything odd about the offer. I didn't even think 'where's Peter Clarke?' Nowadays, Percy would probably have to explain himself to the police and I would be taken into care.

The occasion was Saturday, 15 October 1960, versus Queens Park Rangers. Real Madrid was the team of the moment in 1960, following their extraordinary 7-3 European Cup Final victory over Eintracht Frankfurt the previous May. QPR played in all white and did a passable impression of Real Madrid, winning the game 1-0, with a goal from their burly Welsh centre-forward, Brian Bedford. Years later I was introduced to Mr Bedford in a London pub by the father of a friend. I told him the story and said 'let me buy you a drink'. 'Son,' he replied, 'in the circumstances I think I ought to buy you a drink.' I therefore took him off my list of Totally Irrational Hatreds in Football.

There is something entirely appropriate in beginning my Vale-watching career with a defeat. One of the familiar tropes about sport is that it teaches people how to deal with disappointment. This is rubbish. Lots of people never learn to deal with defeat. Some defeats rankle forever. The world is full of bad losers, who turn to violence and drink, stew in self-pity, hide in darkened rooms until the pain becomes bearable, or rage against the unfairness of it all, especially against the 'bastards in the black/green/yellow/red'. In very bad cases, of course, they rage against their own players, who just don't care as much as they should do, as much as the fans do. As my old friend Richard Szreter, a Baggies' fan, used to say, 'the true fan loves the club and hates the team'. I treasure the memory of a train journey from Stoke with a group of Japanese who had been to see the Mighty Reds at Old Trafford. Unaccountably, the Mighty Reds had lost. Some of the Japanese looked to be contemplating ritual suicide; others had the astonished and angry demeanour of people who had saved up and travelled round the world to eat at a Michelin-starred restaurant only to be served powered egg and oven chips. I often wonder if they are still in therapy.

I tasted victory for the first time at my second game. This time I went with Peter Clarke. We stood behind the goal at the Bycars End and spent most of the match generating a fearful racket by banging on the corrugated iron at the back of the stand. (Anyone trying this now would assuredly be invited to desist or leave the ground.) The game was against Southend United. The Vale won 4-0. I was surprised that I could remember who scored the first goal I saw the Vale concede but not the first one I saw them score. I had to look it up. I was even more surprised to see that it was Bert Llewellyn, who was my first Vale Hero.

The Vale were the first team to win the newly-formed Division 4 in 1959 and played a lot of nice football during the early 1960s under Norman Low, occasionally threatening promotion but always falling away in the final stretch. A game against Shrewsbury Town on Good Friday 1963 haunts me still. I remember everyone saying that we needed five points from the hectic three-game Easter schedule to sustain our promotion push: Shrewsbury Town at home; Queens Park Rangers away; and Shrewsbury Town away. We got the one point we didn't want, a nil nil draw in the home game against Shrewsbury. We absolutely murdered them. Arthur Rowley was their player manager. He must have set some kind of record for clearing balls off the line. Boy, did he have a left foot and when he cleared a ball it stayed cleared. He became the second of my Totally Irrational Hatreds in Football. I am sure that Rowley was a very decent man and a very fine player, but I still remember him principally for the pain he inflicted on me that day. I know I should have got over it by now, but I haven't. It is always good to beat Shrewsbury. 1963 was as close as we got in my youth to a Return to Camelot. We finished third in Division 3, but only two clubs were promoted in those days. The five points we failed to secure over Easter would have seen us finish second. We were relegated in 1965. This was the prelude to one of the most extraordinary periods in Port Vale history.

Enter Sir Stanley Matthews. The great man became Vale 'general manager' in July 1965. He immediately established a youth policy and some of the cream of young British football talent flocked to Vale Park. Hope soared. Hope is a dangerous commodity. The nearest I have come to living without football hope was recently, in the dire 2008-9 season. As my friend Mick Rowson observed, watching the Vale that season was like seeing someone torture to death a much-loved pet. When Micky Adams took over in the summer of 2009 someone asked him if he had seen the Vale play the previous season. He replied that he had not. At this point an elderly Vale fan interjected, 'no bugger saw the Vale play last season'. No truer words have ever been spoken. 'Abject doesn't even begin to describe it. So no hope is bad. But too much hope is possibly even worse. The arrival of Matthews and a phalanx of young talent propelled expectations into the stratosphere. They were given substance by a good run in the FA Youth Cup, when we lost (unglamorously) in (I think) the quarter-final to Scunthorpe United, who lost in the semi-final to Arsenal, the eventual winners. If you support, say Chelsea, you must get used to jealousy, but it is unusual for fans to be jealous of the Vale. But Matthews had that effect, too. On my way home from the Scunthorpe game I was set upon by some Stokies who had also been to the game, presumably to support The Iron. One tried to grab my scarf. This is the footballing equivalent of losing a regimental standard during the Napoleonic Wars, so I did what any right thinking Englishman would do in the circumstances. I lamped the Stokie in the ear with a cracking left hook and legged it. I think part of me knew then that the Matthews Era was going to end in tears. The team did not blossom. In the 1965-66 season we finished 19th in Division 4, 13th in 1966-67, 18th in 1967-68. In February and March 1968 the club was fined £4,000 and expelled from the Football League for 'financial irregularities'. I was in my first year at university and I became incoherent with a sense of helplessness. For a while it looked as though the club might fold. That it did not owed much to the favours called in by Sir Stan and by his willingness to forego substantial sums owed to him. Nothing in his time at the club lived up his leaving of it.

Out of this mess came a hero – Gordon Francis Lee. I would never have expected a Vale saviour to come from Shrewsbury, but that is where Lee had been working prior to his appointment as Vale manager in May 1968. This was the time when European youth was ablaze with revolutionary fervour. A few years ago a student asked me what it was like in 'May '68'. I replied that it was 'a great moment in history. Gordon Lee became Port Vale manager'. Most Vale fans will put John Rudge at the top of their managerial list, and understandably so, but Lee is my all-time favourite. He was only 34 when he took over. It was immediately evident that he belonged to a new generation of coaches. Like a lot of excellent managers, he was not an especially good player. I had complete faith in him. Tactically, he was by far the best Vale manager (except, perhaps, for the first coming of Freddie Steele), better than Rudge in my view. Ray Harford once told me that Lee was the best tactical manager he had ever known. Lee turned a group of average players, some of very limited skill, into a promotion winning side in the 1969-70 season. If I could live one year of my life over again, 1969-70 would certainly make the shortlist. The autumn of 1969 was one of the finest of the century. It was my last year at university, ending in academic triumph. And I was in love. I managed to fit in most of the games that season, home and away, and never doubted that we would go up. The decisive game came at Notts County on 8 April, my sister's birthday. The Vale won 2-1, with – fittingly – a goal from Roy Sproson, last playing survivor of the great team of '54. (As a supporter I have lucky grounds and unlucky grounds. Notts County is one of the luckiest. I have never seen Vale lose there. Last season it was the occasion of one of Vale's worst performances after which Micky Adams put all the players on the transfer list. Honest, Micky it wasn't their fault. It was mine. I was unable to get to the game. If I'd been there we would have won. Don't even ask about Bolton, Brentford, Crewe, Oldham, Tranmere, Walsall,

Watford, York and, worst of all, Luton. If I turn up at any of these places defeat is inevitable.)

The Vale team of 1969-70 is often dismissed as 'workmanlike'. The veteran BBC Merseyside football reporter, Bill Bothwell, memorably described as 'an out of breath Scotsman', actually stigmatised the team as 'the Port Vale musclemen'. He went straight into my little black book. This epithet could not be applied to the star of the team, John Green, one of five men who were ever-present during the season (which is a round-about-way of showing that we didn't get many suspensions). Modern midfield players are often all about physicality and athleticism, Michael Essien for example. John Green was different. I have never seen a player who seemed to put less physical effort into his game (yes, even Berbatov). Green did not move, he materialised. His weapon was not strength or speed or trickery, it was the ball.

I don't suppose the penultimate game of the 1974-75 season, played on Saturday, 26 April, will stir many memories with most Vale fans, but it marked one of the low points in my football odyssey. 1974-75 was not a bad season. We finished sixth in Division 3 and were pushing for promotion much of the time. So were the team we played on 26 April, Blackburn Rovers, who gave us a royal going over, winning 4-1, a victory that helped them secure the divisional title. What made this defeat painful was the name of the Blackburn manager, Gordon Lee. Whenever Port Vale has a good manager he has invariably to feed off scraps. Whenever we come into any money we inevitably give it to someone who will waste it. (John Rudge is the exception to both these statements.) If ever there was a manager you could trust with money it was Gordon Lee. Once he moved to Blackburn he bought all the players he tried and failed to get for the Vale. If anyone was ever going to return us to Camelot it was Gordon Lee and we had blown it. I could have cried. I probably did cry. I went straight from the game to play tennis. I was so upset I could barely hold the racket.

After the recent game against Shrewsbury Town (28 September 2010) I was being given a lift back to the station in a friend's car. We were listening to the phone-in on BBC Radio Stoke (definitely Radio Stoke and not Radio Vale), when a Vale fan announced that 'the last seventeen minutes of the game were the longest of my life'. I just guffawed. No Vale fan who was not present at the Play-Off Final Second Leg against Bristol Rovers on Saturday, 3 June 1989, has any right to express an opinion about the nature of time. The last twenty minutes were eternal, the last five minutes excruciating. All I can remember is a cacophony of whistling that drowned out spirited renditions of 'Goodnight Irene' from the wonderful Rovers fans. (You could see their lips moving in song, but you couldn't hear anything above the whistling.) The most iconic Vale image ever for me, beating even Dean Glover receiving the Autoglass Trophy at Wembley from Bobby Charlton, is that of Robbie Earle sitting, head bowed, completely spent, at the entrance to the players' tunnel after the Play-Off Final. (Never mind Dutch girls and World Cup tickets, Robbie, you're OK in my book.) When the whistle went and we had won and were back to the Promised Land from which the great team of '54 were expelled in 1957, I cried. I cried over my children. I cried over my best friend, Brian Shirley, and then went home and cried over my dad. But before I got home I had a promise to fulfil. I told the boys that if we won I would buy them both Vale kits. We went straight into a deserted Burslem and got them fitted out. Once the emotion had subsided, Tom, wearing his spanking new strip, and I went to get some fish and chips. Just after we set foot in the shop the Bristol Rovers team bus pulled up outside. Their kitman came in to buy fish and chips for the team (and a very nice chap he was). I am not proud of what happened next. 'Look, Tom,' I said, 'why don't you go outside and give Mr Francis and his players a wave.' He complied. Not a player returned his wave, not even with a 'V' sign. They just looked bereft. I have had a soft spot for the Gasheads ever since.

Inappropriately, perhaps, for a club with strong Methodist roots, the Return to Camelot began on a Sunday, though there was no way of knowing that at the time. It was the

ThirdRound of the FA Cup against (then) Non-League Macclesfield Town. (Little clubs, like Port Vale, often get hacked off by the condescension of bigger clubs and their smug fans. But there's always a club smaller than you and I have often been ashamed at the attitude of Vale fans towards clubs like Accrington Stanley, Macclesfield Town and Morecambe in recent seasons. They really ought to know better.) Vale were not doing well in the League in January 1988 and we did not play well against Macclesfield, but won with a cracking goal from Kevin Finney. Finney was one of those all-too-familiar players who very occasionally look like a world beater, great movement, great first touch, good finisher, but who clearly had Something Missing. Even so, his goal in this game assures him a place in the Vale Panetheon. It possibly saved the Vale career of John Rudge. And it put us into the hat for the FA Cup Fourth Round, when we drew the holders, Tottenham Hotspur, at home. This had echoes of Blackpool in 1954.

The victories over Blackpool and Spurs had one thing in common. They were both accomplished on very heavy pitches. Spurs' defeat still rankles with their fans. Their usual excuse is that 'Port Vale watered the pitch'. Believe me, there was no need to water it. God did a very good job. I felt unusually tense the morning of the game and went for a walk in the vicinity of the ground, which has fields at the back and a park across the road from the front. Everywhere was absolutely sodden. This knowledge did not comfort me. My thought was not 'oh, good, super Spurs' silky skills will be no use on this mudheap'. It was 'there's no way the Vale will be able to play on this mudheap'. But we did. We won the game because Ray Walker and Robbie Earle (just returned from a long injury lay off) bossed the midfield and Phil Sproson defended like a man with Vale in his DNA. Chris Waddle put in a fine performance for Spurs, but we only really started coming under pressure in the second half when Gary Mabbutt began to make surging runs from the back. And then Master Tactician Terry Venables took Mabbutt off. I have had my doubts about El Tel ever since. The win over Spurs virtually re-invented the club, gave old fans hope and brought new ones to the ground. Above all, perhaps, it gave the team belief. We finished a respectable eleventh in 1988 and were promoted the following season.

Promotion to Division 2 (aka Division 1, aka The Championship) also launched the Golden Age of John Rudge. It is usually in the nature of Golden Ages that they are not recognised until they are over. This was not the case with the Rudge Era. I knew it was a Golden Age. Possibly everyone else knew it was a Golden Age. The Rudge Era was not all jam. There were relegations as well as promotions and cup runs. My dad always told me that all I could do was my best and if my best was not good enough then tough. This is generally good advice, especially when your best is good enough, at least most of the time. But there were two seasons in the second tier of English football under Rudge when the team was simply out of its depth. No matter how well it played, it lost. Games, especially at home, had a demoralising predictability about them. Vale would play neat football, dominate possession for ten, twenty, forty, even sixty minutes, but they would fail to score, then concede and duly lose. But this is not how the Rudge Era is remembered, nor how I remember it. I said to my sons that we were unlikely ever to have such a good team again (I'm not sure they believed me) and that we had to go to as many games as possible and enjoy it while it lasted.

There were many golden moments during the Rudge Era and in the memory they out dazzle the dross: the Autoglass Trophy win at Wembley on 22 May 1993, especially the glorious first-half (when Lennie Lawrence, Sky Sports pundit for the game, declared that 'Port Vale are playing like AC Milan'); the FA Cup victories over Derby County, Southampton and Everton (cup holders at the time); competing successfully with clubs like Manchester City, Wolves, West Brom, Birmingham City and (yes) Stoke City; wonderful, memorable goals, especially from Tony Naylor, an artist among goalscorers, especially perhaps his superb goals against Sunderland at home and Manchester City away, the sweeping move resulting in a devastating finish by Nicky Cross against the Baggies at the Hawthorns, Andy Porter's winner in the same game, Porter's goal against Stoke in the epic FA Cup replay, played in monsoon conditions at Vale Park, and Martin Foyle's *coup de grace*. Rudge assembled some of the best players ever to wear the Vale shirt: Neil Aspin; Darren Beckford; Robbie Earle; Dean Glover; Martin Foyle; Steve Guppy; Andy Jones; Jon McCarthy; Andy Porter; Peter Swan; Ian Taylor; Robin van der Laan; Ray Walker. Listing them is both uplifting and depressing.

The official high water mark of the Rudge Era was the 8th place finish in The Championship in 1997, the club's highest finish since 1931. With three games to go we were in with a shout of the Play-Offs, but two galling defeats, one to Stoke City, away, and one to Wolves, at home, ended that impossible dream. But for me the high water mark came in the previous season. This was the season we had a great run after Christmas, the year we beat Everton in the FA Cup and reached the final of the Anglo-Italian Cup, our third Wembley visit under Rudge. Once again Easter proved fateful. We played Birmingham City away on Easter Saturday. The Blues had not been playing well and Barry Fry's team selection had erred at times on the side of the bizarre. I will never forgive him for what he did that day. He picked a well-balanced team in a recognisable formation. Vale looked very tired and lost 3-1. On Easter Monday we played Oldham Athletic at home. Although our away record at Boundary Park is abject, we usually beat Oldham at home. When we don't it is because the Gods are trying to tell you something. We duly lost that day, to a goal scored by Darren Beckford, of all people. Sport is cruel. I remember walking out of the ground at the end thinking 'downhill all the way after this'. This clearly failed to predict the achievements of the following season, but it was right in spirit.

Someone said that all managerial careers end in failure. I don't know a single Vale fan who thinks that John Rudge should have been sacked. As my friend Peter Simkins said, 'you'll be OK as long as you've got Rudgie'. I learned of his dismissal in a phone call from my younger son. All I could say was 'bloody hell'. The end of the Rudge Era was not the end of good times. We won the LDV Vans Trophy at the Millennium Stadium on a very wet day in 2001 and had a very good team in which Dave Brammer and Marc Bridge-Wilkinson starred. (It is noticeable that the success Vale enjoyed under John Rudge and Brian Horton was marked by the presence of a goalscoring midfielder, something we have lacked for a long time.) But since then times have been hard, with mediocrity on the pitch and financial travail off it. There seemed no end in sight to the downward spiral until the appointment of Micky Adams, who has at least given us a team that is fit and well-organised. For the first time in ages Vale fans are looking forward instead of back.

When we troop off to the football, my wife invariably says 'enjoy yourselves'. We shake our heads, knowingly. Football is not about enjoyment, at least not for me. Enjoyment is a far too trivial, superficial feeling to embrace the emotional roller-coaster that is football. If your team is pushing for honours, your life is filled with tension and anxiety. If your team is rubbish and plunging towards relegation, your life is filled with tension and anxiety. If your team is mired in mid-table mediocrity your life is filled with dismay and frustration. A sensible person would take up flower arranging (very relaxing, so I am told). I am not a sensible person. As my friend Brian Shirley says, 'some people don't understand that football is not really about football'. For me, it is about identity, memory, family, loyalty. I once heard someone say that 'Port Vale fans are people who have no ambition'. I had to restrain a powerful desire to disembowel him. Presumably, ambitious people leg it up the road to Manchester and associate themselves with a 'winning brand'. Supporting Port Vale has taught me many things. First, things are never so bad that they can't get worse. Second, that the only rational approach to existence is pessimism of the intellect and optimism of the spirit. Third, that the very survival of clubs like Port Vale has been miraculous. Although we are a country that prides itself on longevity and tradition, there are not that many businesses more than one hundred years old. Port Vale was a product of the late nineteenth century urban working-class culture and of religious non-conformity. Both these things are now at one with Nineveh and Tyre. The club has survived extraordinary events and extraordinary social change, the pace of which gets ever faster and a financial climate that becomes ever more challenging. Football and football supporters are often very unappealing, filled with hate, aggression, violence, intolerance, jingoism and drink. But this is not why football clubs survive. It is because people love them. Ironically, the people who love them most are the ones with the least influence on their destinies. Even the supporters of great and big clubs are beginning to realise this. Liverpool fans already have. Manchester United is surely a train crash waiting to happen. I take no joy in this.

If this journey has been an Odyssey, does that make me Ulysses? And, like him, am I destined:

To sail beyond the sunset, and the baths
Of all the western stars, until I die.
It may be that the gulfs will wash us down:
It may be we shall touch the Happy Isles,
And see the great Achilles, whom we knew.
Tho' much is taken, much abides; and though
We are not now that strength which in old days
Moved earth and heaven; that which we are, we are;
One equal temper of heroic hearts,
Made weak by time and fate, but strong in will
To strive, to seek, to find, and not to yield.

Or, more prosaically, Vale 'til I die! And beyond the grave!

11

Bath City

What Did the Romans do to Me?

Gerry Dolan

Was it Portland United or Merthyr Tydfil at Twerton Park? It certainly wasn't Clifton or Old Merchants Taylors at the Recreation Ground! After all these years I can't remember which was the first Bath City game that my Dad took me to see. That's how it all began for most of us I think. Mums didn't go to football matches then. Times have changed since the 1960s and while for many it can be a family occasion, it will often be Dad who has the greatest influence on the son as to which team he will be saddled with following for the rest of his life. I do sometimes wonder what it would have been like to have been taken to the home of Bath Rugby at the Recreation Ground and by now having celebrated a European Cup, top flight league and national cup wins. That would have been good no doubt about that, but football was always going to be my game I suppose. Dad was a fan and while he did watch the rugby occasionally, it was to Twerton Park that he went regularly. He was a teacher and doubled up as a part time reporter for the local paper The Bath Chronicle and reported on the Bath Boys schools team. There were several players that went through to the City set up and he would inevitably monitor their progress.

He often talked about 'the' home game against Bolton Wanderers in the FA Cup Third Round in 1964, before I started going. His main claim was that it gave him lumbago which kept him off work for several days! Bolton was a very reputable top flight team in those days, even more than they are now. Malcolm Allison was the City manager that season and it was only a late Francis Lee penalty that saw the Lancashire team escape with a draw and go on to win the replay in front of over 27,000 fans. It was four more years before I can remember going regularly, a night game at Twerton Park in front of over 2,000 fans against Salisbury that I can definitely remember being at a game. I can recall flags and banners, the unique atmosphere that only a game under lights can bring, the bustle of the crowd from the stand (we would always sit down!), and we won. It was not always going to be like that....

My early days followed a three year period where City went down, up and down again from the Southern League Premier Division, though reached the Second Round of the FA Cup in two of those seasons. In those days the Southern League was acknowledged as the premier non-league competition outside the Football League. Its equivalent in the north, the Northern Premier League, would shortly come into existence in 1968 to bring together semi-professional football in the north and provide rivals for election to the Football League for that is how it was before the automatic promotion came about in 1987. City were a strong side in the late 50s and early 60s but now they were inconsistent and it would be not until the late 1970s that they would regain their place at the top of the Southern League again.

In the early part of that decade and in my formative supporting years it was all about following the team, game by game, watching the table of course, but no real feel for the strategy of what the club was going through, how the finances were, what the future holds. We had moved from Bath to Hertfordshire before I was eight years old yet that didn't seem to dim my enthusiasm, if anything the distance enhanced it. It was a bit daunting trailing my Bath City FC sports bag into an Enfield school full of Spurs and Arsenal fans, particularly when we weren't gracing any national stage in the FA Cup. I like to think my own football ability in the school team made me immune from any would be bullying that might have happened.

The Salisbury game was in the promotion season that saw the club back in the Southern Premier but a steady decline followed and in 1972 relegation happened again. That season was odd in the team didn't score many goals (45 in 42 games) but forward John Mitten, transferred from Exeter City, got 19 of them, almost three times more than the next highest scorer. For me he was the star player then in a mediocre team. My first hero! The record shows that City lost eight successive league games in March and April, bad run, wrong time, confirmed relegation.

City had a proud FA Cup record but after a period of regularly appearing in the FA Cup First Round, they were about to go into a period of 16 years where they only reached the First Round twice. In those days exemptions in the competition depended on how well you performed in the previous years, not in which League you played. So City would often line up against local, lower league teams in the early rounds who saw this as their Cup Final...and would often come away with the silverware.

The Club's rise back to the echelon of the non-league game began with the arrival of a new manager and a new kit. Dave Burnside was installed as manager in August of 1972 and the former West Bromwich Albion playmaker, and ball juggler, installed the Baggies' famous blue and white stripes as the Club colours. It wasn't to be a perfect match for the manager or the kit. A 6-2 home defeat to the Met Police in January 1973 saw Burnside relieved of his post and new man Roy Bence installed. The team recovered to finish 7th. The team played 67 games that season as the Club entered six competitions including the newly formed FA Trophy which had replaced the Amateur Cup and gave, for the first time, semi-professional clubs their own competition and a chance to play at Wembley. However it was a competition City would never do well in and dreams of Wembley, even with better teams in future years, were never more than a pipe dream.

Promotion the following year was clinched in the final two games both against Andover, 6-0 at home and I remember jigging around the lounge when news came through on the phone (how else for non-league football in the 70s??) of Tony Gough's strike to send City back into the top tier again. If we thought 67 games was a lot then the 92 that the team played in 1974/75 now seems unbelievable. Deciding that six competitions didn't fill all the time available they added an extra three, with eight players playing more than 50 games. Colin Tavener, a legendary full back who had played in Hereford United's great Cup team two years previously, played 78 games. Another hero for me, I can't remember ever seeing him lose the ball or pass to the opposition no matter how tight or how many people around him, he had a magical left foot.

That season of 1974/75 under another new manager Bert Head saw the beginnings of a side that would bring City the title three years later. The highlight of that season however was a rare appearance in the FA Cup First Round where they lost against a Wimbledon side that went on to hold Leeds away and lose in front of 42,000 at Selhurst Park. I went to both the City game and the Wimbledon-Leeds replay. Plough Lane, where Wimbledon's glory run to the League and top flight football began, saw City take hundreds of supporters who witnessed a cracking game between two sides on top of their game. The only goal, a heart breaker of a 30 yard screamer in the top corner in the last minute from Mick Mahon, will be etched on many a City fan's memory as many of us were right behind the flight line as it swept past Kenny Allen's outstretched arm.

After a hiccough in the 75/76 season that saw City exit the FA Cup in the preliminary round in August at Fareham, one of those names that will make City fans shudder along with Cinderford and Thame in years to come, the appointment of Brian Godfrey in 1976 was a prelude to the most successful City period for over ten years. Winning the first four games gave City fans hope of greater things to come and although they eventually finished fourth to another rampant Wimbledon team, despite doing the double over them, and suffering another first game exit from the FA Cup, it was clear that there was a team forming that were exciting, confident, and most important of all, successful. The fact City only entered seven competitions with a maximum of 58 games on offer must have clearly helped to have provided greater rest and focus! An eight game unbeaten League run at the end of the season provided the momentum for a season that many City fans still rate as the best ever.

As with all great seasons you can always remember a lot more about the games, more easily pick out the highlights, indeed think the whole season was one big glory trail. The Southern League Championship season of 1977/78 had all of that as well as some bizarre scorelines. A twenty-nine game unbeaten run from the start of the season until the middle of March laid the foundations. A fair few draws but important wins against key teams none more so than the 7-2 Boxing Day demolition of eventual runners up Weymouth on their own ground. The following day (yes in those days there was little breathing space) City played out a 4-4 draw against a Cheltenham team that they were to share no fewer than twenty-two goals in the season. A crazy 7-1 defeat in the FA Trophy was avenged by a 6-0 win the in the league reverse.

The 4-4 draw saw an erratic display by City goalkeeper legend Kenny Allen. A 6ft 4in commander of the penalty area City were not to see the likes again for almost thirty years. Seemingly able to suck and pluck the ball into his giant hands from crosses, he also had fans in states of despair at some elementary handling mistakes, but he was a key figure in this great season. Almost twenty clean sheets, best defence in the League, the Cheltenham 4 was the culmination of conceding ten goals in four successive games in December, he more than made up for it by only conceding ten in the remaining twenty-six games.

Five days later I sat in the cavernous stand at Rockingham Road, the home of Kettering Town, listening to Daddy Cool echo around the ground ahead of City's New Year game. It was a cameo of the season. Tight defence, taking the opportunities when they came, and in the little Scot Andy Provan they had one of the sharpest goal poachers around. He won the game from inside the box, I don't think he scored many from outside! So the points continued to roll in, however, at only two points for a win City were never seemingly that clear. After drawing with Weymouth in front of over 3,000 at Twerton Park, and rolling over a Barnet side with Jimmy Greaves, City arrived at Leamington's Windmill Ground on the last Friday in April for their penultimate game of the season knowing a win would give them only their second ever Southern League title almost twenty years after the first. Why a Friday? Perhaps the FA Trophy final was on the Saturday? Who knows? Who cares now? My Dad and I found our way to Leamington with hundreds of other City fans to witness our crowning glory. We were not disappointed. A 2-0 win clinched the title and scenes in the clubhouse the like of which is only seen when titles are won, people are happy, and dreams are fulfilled. We only lost two league games that season, drew with a table topping Plymouth Argyle at home in the FA Cup, and enjoyed success in the Anglo Italian tournament which pitted us against teams from the Italian Serie C, probably better than the Southern League and equivalent competitions in this country. City lost to Udinese in the final who are now an established Serie A side, contain many internationals, and have now graced the UEFA Champions League. City could only dream of reaching such a level, but perhaps that dream might have taken a gigantic step forward if they had been elected to the Football League at the end of the season. Southport were the team under threat as City and Wigan Athletic were the non-league challengers. City lost out with the highest number of votes polled by an unsuccessful team. Wigan were elected after an initial tie. Whatever happened to them....

Changes were happening in non-league football at the end of the 1970s as clubs realised that they needed to form a single national league if they were going to present a creditable nominee to get into the League. Clubs coming from north and south were simply dividing the vote and few teams were being elected, Wigan being the last. So the Alliance Premier League was born with clubs from both the Southern and Northern Premier League. The Isthmian League, the third major non-league - comprising clubs largely around the London area - refused to join in as they saw the national League relegating their competition's importance. They came around eventually and allowed the likes of Enfield and Dagenham to take their place. Eligibility was based on league placement and City easily qualified finishing fourth in 1979. City made their bow in the initial twenty team league at Boston United's impressive York Street ground and a difficult debut season ended in comfortably avoiding relegation. Brian Godfrey had gone in the middle of the previous season to Exeter City and Bob Boyd was in charge for the initial season.

City's move into the national arena was matched by my own job move into pastures new from London to Luton. While I settled in to the area over the next few years, so City consolidated in the new League. Never setting it alight but never in danger of going down, or in danger of getting to the First Round of the FA Cup! This was the era of former Bristol Rovers star Bobby Jones at the helm of City. He was to be there for six years during this period of gradual improvement. In 1985 but for a bizarre points scoring system City would have won what was now called the Gola League. It was in the middle of a three year experiment with awarding two points for a home win and three points for an away win. If it had been three points for all wins, City's phenomenal fifteen home wins would have put them in top spot. It is one of the freak scenarios that fans can point to when they lament the bad luck that haunts their team. I guess it all evens it self out, but how long do you have to wait??

Perhaps the disappointment of that still highest ever finish in their non-league history affected everyone as City then began a slide down the table that was to lead to relegation. This contrasted with City's improving fortunes in the FA Cup where they got to the Second Round three times and the Thirdround once. 1986 saw defeat at Peterborough in the Second Round and the following year two games against Bristol City in front of a combined attendance of almost 20,000 saw Paul Bodin give City a replay with a volley that fans have rated one of the best ever City goals. In 1988 City won three Cup games to get to the ThirdRound for the first time in twenty-five years. The Cup draws then were still on Monday lunchtime, so, working back in London, I brought in my radio and listened to the draw being made by those august FA members. It could have been anyone, big names then were still Man Utd, Arsenal, Liverpool....but not Mansfield. It was to Field Mill in a Death without Glory game that City had to go to. Along with many games in the 80s, I didn't get to go as I was playing myself in the humble surrounds of the Spartan and Herts County Leagues. Suffice to say we lost 4-0 at Mansfield, dream over.

And life in the what was then the Vauxhall Conference had ended as well in 1988. A year after Scarborough gained the first automatic promotion place, City filled the final relegation place as Lincoln City returned to the League at the first attempt. Bobby Jones went at the end of the season and it all seemed that an era had ended. How would we deal with the Southern League again? The following season gave little clue to the drama to come shortly as City flirted with another relegation to eventually pull clear. Fareham were relegated with 51 points from 42 games. City were given a bye to the First Round of the FA Cup and squandered a two goal lead in the Second Round to Welling which would have given them a tie with an up and coming Blackburn Rovers side. It was a 62 game season as City went for seven competitions including the boundaryless Welsh Cup. Oh, and there were four managers as well!

The start of the 1989/90 season saw George Rooney installed as City boss. Rooney had been a journeyman manager but turned out to be exactly the right person at exactly the right time. He was also perhaps fortunate to have retained a player signed in April for a few games at the back end of that season. That player was Paul Randall who became a City legend, the second all time top scorer, and has a bar named after him at Twerton Park.

The 69 games City played that season saw them celebrate success on a number of fronts but only win the Somerset Premier Cup in terms of silverware. The League became a war of attrition between three teams, City, Dover and Dartford. All three seemed to win week in week out and it was only City's 1-0 away win at Watling Street in April that finally saddled Dartford with third place. I remember cheering the City coach as it was leaving the ground, flushed with an unlikely success that kept us right in the title race, but also flushed in the cheeks because it was cold standing outside my broken down car waiting for the AA man to come and fix it.

A week later and defeat at Worcester effectively ended City's title bid, finishing with a record breaking 98 points from 42 games, still four points behind Dover despite having taken four points of them. Randall scored 51 goals in all, 36 in the League including three hat tricks and a brace seven times. And only three penalties. At one stage City won fourteen successive League games, just shows what Dover were doing on the south coast! However, the real drama was yet to come as rumours had been floating around that Dover's Crabble ground was not up to the standard required for promotion to the Conference. They were making very positive noises that all work would be done before next season, however, the due date was considerably earlier than that. As I was holidaying in Spain aware that the FA were due to make a decision, hunting down UK papers for the news, until a small article appeared in the Daily Telegraph that had me, once again, jigging away this time down the streets of Palma to bewildered looks from Spanish and tourists alike – Dover had been refused promotion, and City as runners up has taken their place! Relations between the two sides have been strained since, specifically as allegedly a City fan sent them a few pennies (literally) towards ground improvements!

The roller coaster League was only part of the season's story. Unusually our good Cup runs were interspersed with League success. Jimmy Hill wasn't looking forward to his beloved Fulham taking on City in the First Round of the FA Cup as his side came back from two down to take us back to Craven Cottage. I had been on a weekend break in the New Forest with what would be my next wife, but was available for the replay, and along with hordes of City fans we made our way along the Thames. City took an early lead but though eventually losing 2-1 put up a tremendous effort and were visibly the fitter of the two sides towards the end. It was also City's best ever season in the FA Trophy. After winning through four rounds to the quarter-finals and the genuine hope of Wembley in our minds, perennial Trophy success team Stafford Rangers burst the bubble with a 2-0 win at Twerton.

City's now seemingly regular seven competition entry approach had seen progress on all fronts and it was some reward that Dave Singleton notched the winner against Taunton in early May to give City the County Cup and some silverware for the Board room. Singleton was a fashionably moody player who could mix flair with the ugly side of the game in equal and sometimes unequal measure. Never shy of a put down, I made the mistake early one season of saying I had scored more goals than he had (albeit at different levels of course!), to which he replied that he reckoned that he'd had more women than me! Which if course he probably had. I still can't think what a response to that might be. Nor could my Dad, who was with me at the time!

City's return to the top level of non-league football was a reality check as they found defences far less accommodating than in the Southern League. Randall was still banging in the goals, alas so was the opposition as City struggled to keep clear of the bottom two and relegation. I recall a Tuesday night at Sutton in March where icon Graham Withey grabbed what turned out to be a precious point. Withey has been one of those players, unlike Randall, who has divided opinion among City supporters over the years, and there have been plenty of years as Withey has seemingly made umpteen returns. Indeed, if he trotted out in a City shirt now I think most fans would only be mildly surprised. Another player with the ability to enthral and enrage, Withey was a tall, solidly built player who when on song showed why he played at a higher level with Bristol Rovers and Coventry. At his worst he would struggle for a place at Lansdown on a Sunday morning. One classic episode saw him break free towards the Barnet goal, yet get himself sent off within ten seconds, as he first overran the ball, lost it to the keeper, and gave such a verbal volley to the referee that a red card was the only option. To be fair, I would say that in terms of target men, City have seldom seen much better.

The Sutton point was the first for new manager City centre back Tony Ricketts who stepped up as player manager to try and stave off relegation when Rooney was given the axe. And that is what he did. Two defeats in thirteen games before the penultimate game that saw a draw at Merthyr Tydfil were enough to keep City in the top flight and consolidate Ricketts in his post that was to see a period of comfortable finishes in the Conference and great cup success. By 1990 Bristol Rovers had been ground sharing with City for four years and were enjoying much success in League and Cup in their new home in front of large crowds. This helped ensure City had both a League standard ground able to accommodate large Cup crowds as well as provide a boost to the playing budget through the rental payments. When Ricketts started to build his squad in 1991 it was, to my mind, one of the best teams that I have ever seen during my support of the club. The strength, power, and confidence within the team along with Ricketts's utter determination and single mindedness meant City fans were to enjoy some great Cup success and national exposure.

Ricketts's first job was to harness the guile of Randall with the aerial ability of Withey to give a front two capable of scoring enough in the Conference to give a City a better chance of an easier season. His second was to get another season about of Chris Banks who for me, pound for pound, must be just about the classiest player I have ever seen don a City shirt. Chris was about to embark on the third of his five seasons with City that saw him play over 250 games. A virtual ever present and probably the first name on the teamsheet, Banks was one of those players that you would always want on your side and would grudgingly admire if on the other. A tough tackler when required, controlled the defence superbly alongside player manger Ricketts and was always adept and setting players free as City built a formidable defence (Ricketts was after all a defender!). City finished a comfortable 9th but it was as if we were being served an aperitif for the following seasons where City achieved unparalleled success in the modern era in the FA Cup before, just as easily, events off the field were to force them into a thirteen year wilderness from the top flight.

1992/93 was going to be a strange old season. If City fans had been told that a centre half would finish as leading scorer we would have feared the worst. If we had also been told that a journeyman midfielder who served to both delight and dismay would have scored 10 goals from 12 starts and 16 sub appearances then we would have been truly fearful. This was the season of defender come hot shot Richard Crowley and the enigma that was Deion Vernon. City only scored two goals in the first six league games and languished near the bottom. Randall was injured and though would only score seven in what was his final season for the club. Nine players would score five or more as everyone chipped in. City's adeptness from set plays led to Crowley scoring regularly, but it was Vernon who had us gasping in admiration or disbelief. A free transfer from Bristol City, Deion could on his day race, wriggle, trick and generally get past defenders so gracefully that you wondered what he was doing with us at this level. On most days you knew exactly why he was with us at this level. Generally used from the bench as an impact player, the idea he would impact positively for us and adversely for the opposition, though not always working like that, Deion had his moments. I saw the match against Farnborough in the November where for perhaps the first and only time, after about ten minutes, I felt so utterly confident that City would win the game I was quite relaxed. They had a confidence, almost arrogance, a complete self belief that they would win. The power of Banks, Crowley, Grantley Dicks, Jerry Gill in defence in front of the ever reliable and all time appearance holder Dave Mogg, the midfield guile of Smart, the strength of the dogs of war Weston, Cousins and Singleton, and sheer brute force of Adie Mings and Withey. There was a streetwise swagger about them that I only associated with the London teams where all the players were called Steve or John. There would be other times when we reverted to country yokel status, rolled over, had out tummys tickled, pockets picked, patted on the head and sent home without any supper or points. Deion took the field as a late sub, where he proceeded to score twice, hit the bar and turn in the performance that would have made any watching scout gawp in admiration. City ran out 5-2 winners.

By November, City had plenty of confidence. They had improved their early season form to such an extent that the following Saturday City went to then high flying Cardiff City in the FA Cup First Round and won 3-2 with Vernon netting the winner. This was, unbelievably for a club with such a proud Cup record, their first win over a League team since a Mike Denton double put away Newport County in 1965. The next round saw them play host to Northampton where a late Randall goal salvaged a 2-2 draw saw a replay at the County Ground they shared with the cricket team. City got hit for three and exited the FA Cup up the pavilion steps.

The following season was one of the most momentous City have ever had. Ricketts kept the nucleus of his strong team, adding in a diminutive forward called Paul Adcock who would make a dream debut with a hat trick in the opening 5-1 win over Macclesfield. A 4-0 win over Kidderminster on August Bank Holiday Monday put City clear top of the Conference. However only one win in their next eleven league games meant the season was destined to end up around mid-table. It was in the FA Cup that City had their date with destiny. They progressed past a couple of rounds to set up a home time against Hereford United, and a tie that Sky thought worthy of putting in front of a national audience live on a Sunday lunchtime. Bath City live on television? Who would have believed it? The actual crowd inside Twerton Park was a respectable 3,000+, it's true to say that over the years City have always got a crowd out for the national competition home and away. First time I can remember having to queue to get into the ground, must have been other times looking at the crowd sizes at the games I have been to.

The game will be long remembered for Paul Batty's winning goal from the edge of the area that curled away from Alan Judge's hands into the top of the net, perfect way for a non-league team to clinch a giant killing. Earlier Nicky Brooks's swept City into the lead after great industry from Adie Mings. Hereford equalised in the second half and then came Batty's winner which Sky still show to this date as a prelude to their

Second Round coverage each year. City and Sky had the result they wanted and both milked the dressing room scenes endlessly. So City into the Third Round for the second time in six years. The prize? Well, away again, this time to Stoke City faring reasonably in the second tier of English football, now known as the Championship. The date was set for the first Saturday in January and City warmed up by doing the double over Yeovil in front of a combined crowd of almost 5,000.

But I had a problem. I was going to Tenerife in January with my wife and 18 month old son. Spanning the Cup match. No way then (1994) of finding any live updates over there, text updates hadn't come of age then. I was stuffed. What had improved was that the papers arrived on the same day. So with great trepidation and accepting that a three-goal defeat was ok I set off to get one from my tropical base. Opened the pages to find plenty of FA Cup Third Round reports, where was it? there! unbelievably we had drawn 0-0. Reading more it appeared Adcock had a great chance to win it. Never mind, a replay at Twerton, and I'm back for it! Next problem, I was back on the weekend before the Tuesday night replay, didn't have the contacts at the club I do now and it was all ticket! And I lived in Dunstable. Family friends in Bath weren't football fans, would they queue up for a ticket? No way. So, the evening arrived and it was torrential rain in both Dunstable and Bath as I listened to Radio 5 provide live updates from the game. Unfortunately in front of a crowd of over 6,000 Stoke won it 4-1, but City had another pay day, and there would be one more but that is the best it would get for quite a few years.

As a remote fan who would travel to games home and away for just the 90 minutes, perhaps some lunch on the way with my Dad when travelling to Bath, my contacts in the Club and news about the Club were limited. No internet or fans forum in those days. I recall phoning up the club for scores and snatching a couple of questions about who scored and how they played. And that was about it. At away games I would sometimes buttonhole a supporter (often dear Bas of the Supporters Club) about the new players, current news, departures, but little about the finances which were to dominate City in the next few years. We even had the weekly paper sent from Bath to Hertfordshire in the 70s so we could keep up with the news. How times have changed these days where, even at a lower level in the non-league, you can get and find news instantly.

The problems for City weren't of the instant variety but they were coming over the hill. City were spending more than they were receiving but as long as Rovers were there the day of reckoning would be deferred.......but Rovers were going to go and no one at City seemed to realise that, or so it seemed from my remote position. City's success in the Cup brought them a bye to the First Round in 1994, and would you believe it they were paired with Rovers at Twerton......well of course it was Twerton, they both played there! This was the final pay day, almost 7,000 in the ground, and five goals in the City net, and one man in an early bath as they were swept aside by what was then a very good Rovers side. For me the game of the season was the 3-0 win over Yeovil on Easter Monday in front of almost 1,200 with probably a good half from South Somerset. Birkby's brace and celebration in front of fans of his former team were a delight. However, even then, as we consigned Yeovil to relegation I felt that with their huge fan base and history they would come back and come back stronger. And they did.

City finished comfortably 12th again but the writing was on the wall and the 1995/96 season started with three straight defeats as players came and went, increased boardroom unrest as mounting debts were revealed, and Rovers finally announced they were off back to Bristol to share with the rugby team. An incredible FA Trophy comeback from two down with ten men against Yeovil to win 3-2 was the highlight. An evergreen Withey winner at Dagenham was the start of three wins on the bounce in late March meant a winless streak of eight games to the end of the season didn't have the devastating effect of relegation that year. However Rovers decision to leave and take away the £60,000 annual rental payments meant City's time in the top tier was numbered. Ricketts had enough and went during the summer. I remember sending a fax to the club telling them in no uncertain terms what I thought of them. Still waiting for the reply.

The summer of 1996 might have had most football eyes focused on England hosting the European Championships, however, for City fans it seemed an exit door had opened at Twerton Park and there was a rush to escape. There can be no harsher reality in non-league football than when the cashflow starts to reduce. Players can sniff this from a long distance and with virtually all on 12 month contracts it was no surprise that many were off to other clubs, not necessarily of an equal or higher status, but that could pay a better wage. Steve Millard, a former player at City and several local clubs, was given the unenviable task of building a team that could survive in the Conference. With the classic mix of a club with little money, energetic youngsters, journeymen pros, and the odd bit of class, City only won three league games before Christmas. A run of six defeats in seven games into the New Year, conceding 24 goals saw City rock bottom and seemingly heading in only one direction. Even the FA Cup had turned against City where, with a player sent off, and drawing at home 0-0 with Cheltenham, many of us had our eyes tuned to Ceefax for the Tuesday night replay which saw City leading 1-0 deep, deep and deeper into injury time. The score wouldn't change or show full time for an age, and then it did......City had lost 4-1 in extra time! Similarly the Trophy teased us with a home 0-0 draw with Stevenage, as in the League game, but a 6-1 tonking in the replay. Stevenage, the new town with London overspill, attitude, arrogance, money, fitter, faster and more athletic players. Another bad day in Stevenage and there have been a few.

Even when the tall, lanky, Witheyesque, Graham Colbourne was signed and scored seven goals in the last twelve league games, it seemed too little too late. So just when the fat lady was singing and we were getting used to the idea of trips to Rothwell and St. Leonards, what do you know, our beloved team only go and put together four wins in five including victories at Halifax and Altrincham to give the football fan the worst of all emotions. Hope. Three wins on the trot including a never to be forgotten 1-0 victory at Hayes with a Colbourne header and keeper Mark Hervin performing heroics as the game seemed to last into Sunday meant this team of ours, this team of bits and pieces, this written off team, this team who would never give in had suddenly put themselves back in the driving seat. Crowds had increased by fifty percent from the start of the season as City fans, true to form, turned out for the relegation battle. That and a promotion in the offing will get the fans out. Mid-table solidarity? Not interested. So with two games left to play it was in our hands. If we won them both Halifax could not catch us. The first was home to Farnborough where a season's best of 1,166 turned up to see City take the lead only for an equaliser to be conceded with eight minutes left. Why did they score? They didn't need the point safe in mid-table. Such unreasonable questions fans ask themselves. So, a win against Northwich and hope Halifax didn't. Of all the teams I would have picked for them, Stevenage would have been right up there. Surely they would make a fist of it. However we had to do our bit, and at 2-0 down at half time it looked like we weren't. Enter Colin Towler. Signed earlier in the season and destined to make almost 250 appearances for the club and become one of the most liked players at Twerton Park, he wasn't the most likely scorer, but score he did, not one but two from centre half as City turned it round in front of almost 1,300 fans going mental as well trying to find out how Halifax were doing. We won, but so did they. Stevenage who had stuffed us had become stuffed. As we trooped onto the pitch and gave the players and Steve Millard a great ovation for their ultimately doomed but oh so brave fight little did I know that it would be 13 years, 2 relationships, 3 accommodations, 4 jobs, and half a dozen cars before City would grace the non-league elite again.

Back in the Southern League it was easier and cheaper. Most of the players stayed, plenty of talk about bouncing back, more wins, but a very hard promotion route. Only one place. The first season also saw Martin Paul, signed the previous season, consolidate his place in the team and start his journey to be City's second all time scorer, usurping Paul Randall. Players fitted the League as they tend to do. Managers know the players that will cut it at that level, and those they are taking a chance on. By and large you need experienced players. City fans have been very faithful, and perhaps too forgiving, over the years to youngsters who try but don't have it at that level. If the only criterion was running through, or into, a brick wall, at times City would have been world class.

Off the field there was better news as finally a supporters consortium took over the Club through the leadership of new Chairman Steve Hall. They set about dealing with the debts and position that the former Board had left the club in. At one stage City were faced with selling Twerton Park to clear debts and move to or build a modest ground that would only take a 1,000 people or so. How close we came to that I don't know but listening to the local radio during working in Bristol it seemed too close for any comfort. A relaunch of the club was celebrated in March 1998 when famous celebrity supporter Ken Loach made film about the club and various fund raisers were put in place. An awkward dismissal of ailing manager Steve Millard took place towards the end of the season and former City player and Welsh international Paul Bodin took over.

The Bodin era lasted three seasons and can be summed up as close but no cigar. Two fourth places before a slide to 15th as the money ran out again. First Nuneaton denied City finishing 23 points clear of second place, City two points further away in a very tight top half which saw only seven points covering second to 11th. Martin Paul was proving a worthy successor to previous legendary City forwards with a 30 goal haul. No Cup success of any sort. The following year was closer. Seven wins in the first eight games put City top with goals shared around the forwards. However, in an unkind irony it was to be City's success from the earlier rounds of the cups that was to prove a decisive factor in the end. Progressing four rounds to the FirstRound of the FA Cup (to lose to Hendon) as well as success in the FA Trophy meant City went six weeks without a League game. Boston took their opportunity and went gathering points. Paul was heading for another 30 goal haul and in January he got a helping hand from a Bristol Rovers loan signing Bobby Zamora. Struggling to shift Jason Roberts and Jamie Cureton from the Rovers line up, Bodin snapped up the young forward. It was to maintain City's challenge and transform Zamora's career. Scoring eight goals in eight appearances - including the League Cup (when you have a loan signing, you maximise his appearances!) - he returned to Rovers, was sold to Brighton for a £100,000, started to score plenty and the rest is history. Still fondly remembered at Twerton Park.

City's challenge had been maintained with a home win over Boston but it was the mid-week games in hand that were to prove crucial. In mid March we went to Rothwell, somewhere in Northamptonshire. The sort of place, ground, and time that only devout non-league fans end up at. Cold, windy, desolate, barren,182 fans present. City came from behind to level and win late on. Dave Mehew volleying the winner prompting a shrieking, banshee style wail from me at their keeper. I think the gist was for him to pick the ball out of the net because that is where we had just stuck it! Only it sounded far worse, and more offensive. Sorry keeper wherever you are. However, there was only to be one more win that season from the last twelve games as the pressure told.

The trough continued in to the next season as City struggled with most of the successful side of the previous two seasons,. A three point deduction after a crucial win over Burton for playing an ineligible player, albeit as a substitute, undermined good work and a promising 6th position in faded to a finishing 15th as City looked disinterested and lost six of the last eight games. It was too much for Bodin with austerity cuts in the offing. He went and City were about to endure their own period in the doldrums, with four successive bottom half positions in the Southern League. Alan Pridham was appointed manager. Clubs by and large appoint managers commensurate with their standing, funds, and ambition. City had appointed Bodin a few years ago in more optimistic times.

They now appointed Pridham. The gulf between the two in football experience was vast, though Pridham did have many contacts and had to use them as players exited and the usual mix of youth and experience was hurried in.

It was around this time that I took a call from Pete McCormack who was a driving force behind raising funds to complete the buy out of the main shareholder at City. The aim was to bring the club back to the supporters, create a Supporters Society with a significant and increasing shareholding that could influence the way the club was run, and protect the club from any threat by a major shareholder without City's interests at heart. I was in a restaurant in Hull at the time, the timing was right for my circumstances, Pete was persuasive, and I was about to do my bit for my club.

It took City eleven games to register a win. A farcical FA Cup defeat against Western League Bideford with keeper Hervin sent off, no sub keeper on the bench, and a forward in goal, seemed symptomatic of the times. City struggled around the fringes of the bottom four. Conceding seven in two games over Christmas meant the new year would be a battle to stay up. The odd win was keeping them afloat along with the goals of Adrian Foster. A player who had been to many clubs, Foster almost single handedly kept the City flag flying. He scored 21 in the season, the next highest was eight. Pound for pound his goals are arguably as valuable as anyone else's in recent times to City's fortunes. However his best was yet to come.

In a sequence designed to test the most ardent fan City proceeded to win alternate games over a period of eleven games in the run in. The others were largely lost, meaning the periods of hope and frustration came and went on a weekly basis. During this run a 4-3 win over Stafford Rangers had the fans experiencing both in a 90 minute cameo of the season. A driving run from centre back Gary Thorne to score epitomised the team's spirit, and Fosters magical close range winning strike and bare chested celebration was as good as it got. Or so we thought at the time. City's ebb and flow meant they came to the final game of the season at Worcester having to win to make certain of staying up. In hindsight, the success of later years can perhaps be directly linked to this game. City were never to sink so low again as they fought their way back up the non-league ladder. Hundreds of City fans went to St. George's Lane to cheer on their team. They got the best possible start as a looping header from Foster - who else - put the City fans in raptures and I vividly recall the roar echoing around the roof of the terraced area we stood in. The rest of the game took forever as these sort of games do, but the last few minutes, or could have been half an hour were played out at a Worcester corner flag as City expertly kept the ball in that area to roars of appreciation from the fans. The whistle went and we won. Streams of City fans were on the pitch because it was all over, we had survived, the world was a better place, and we would learn from this and never experience it again. Well, it's what all fans think at the time, but for City it was the nadir and the recovery could begin.

Pridham deserved to remain at the helm and guided City to a safer position the following season. The highlight was an FA Cup run that comprised two 5-0 wins in early rounds before a tie with Yeovil Town that saw Twerton Park's biggest crowd for years as over 3,400 crammed in (thanks to Maurice Ashman for parking directions!) to see Danny Cleverly volley in a spectacular opener, but miss an easier second as the tie went to a replay and Yeovil run out 3-1 winners. The Cup cash from these and other games allowed City to be confident they could qualify for the new Conference South that would be formed from the top placed teams in the Southern and Isthmian Leagues. All we had to do was finish 13th or better. We didn't. Pridham had recruited former Sunderland player Gary Owers to the team, and when City's position in November was second from bottom Owers took over. One of his early signings was journeyman forward Scott Partridge who had enjoyed a successful goal scoring career with many League clubs. He was to become a City legend. Not yet though as Owers brought City storming back. Partridge scoring 18 goals in 20 league games only for City to lose out to Dorchester in the play-off semi final. The season also had another word etched in City fans minds of Cup defeats, Thame. Wretched 3-0 loss, wretched Dwayne Plummer ripped off his shirt and threw it away. How fans hate that.

The next season, Owers started to put together a team that was to fulfil its potential a few years later. But for 2003/04 it was all about Dunstable and the Cup. I was living in Dunstable then and the idea of my City playing up the road was amazing. But play they did and we won 3-1 and I was home for tea! We played Dunstable again in the FA Trophy a few years later, escaped (the illustrious and articulate Pipeman, Dunstable's multi tasking scribe, gateman, etc, always reminds me that we did) with an injury time equaliser, and won 5-0 in the replay. I went to both and remember Dunstable turning up very late for their replay in their coach run by a company called Three Star. As we saw them arrive from the bar window fifteen minutes after the scheduled kick off time we couldn't help but wonder whether using Five Star would have been a better option!

City had to battle from the first Qualifying Round in the FA Cup and thanks to new signing former Coventry speed merchant John Williams and Partridge they reached the First Round proper. The 'reward' was an away tie at Barnet, then top and setting a scorching pace in the Conference. Early on it looked like we were in for a tough day but Barnet failed to take their chances and we got to the break 0-0. The home team eventually forced a breakthrough and that seemed that, however, it wasn't as Scott Partridge was about to write his name in City folklore with a late double strike that sent City into the Second Round as the lowest ranked team left in the competition. It also sent the hundreds of City fans into rapture, even to the extent of me hugging Ken Loach after the second goal. Such days are what we fans live for, we can forgive so much just to occasionally experience moments like that. The draw took us to Peterborough, an early Williams chance spurned, unsympathetic stewarding, and we exited with a healthy sum generated by the run. The league season didn't pick up and we finished 6th as Histon won it with a lowly 78 points.

2005 saw the appointment of John Relish as manager and Adie Britton as assistant which was to be significant in shaping City's fortunes over the next five years. While former player Steve White was favourite to take over, the experience of Relish and Britton at this level won the day and they proceeded to build the foundations that Gary Owers, who departed to Forest Green Rovers in the summer, had laid. Players like Adie Harris, John Holloway, Gethin Jones, Andy Sandell, were added to the calibre of Paul Evans, Partridge, Jim Rollo, Steve Jones, and Matt Coupe. If Cup success was now going to elude City for a few years, then steady progress in the league was the priority. Tales of three straight wins to kick off the league season was great to hear on my summer holiday in Spain, only to be pegged back at Yate and by Salisbury, and it was the latter that were to plough on relentlessly at the top of the table. City stuttered but came back on track with a timely nine game winning sequence including the mother of comebacks at Banbury where two down became a 3-2 win in mid March to put us top and we began to dream. Not for long as Salisbury won games in hand, we couldn't win at their place (thanks to Pete Flack for the lift), and we had to settle for second. Then we had to settle for nothing as Bedford knocked us out of the play-offs. That feeling of hurt has been often said to have been the spur for the next season. Only winning the league was going to be good enough. City fans were about to enjoy their first title for almost thirty years.

I have finally realised that my relationships are inversely proportional to City's success. Faint heart never won the then love of my life in 1978, a big mistake ended a long relationship at the start of the 2006/07 season, and I let go something very special in 2010. I dread to think the price I will have to pay for City to get to the Football League. Relish had little tinkering to do with his team, but what he did was significant. Chris Holland became a fixture. Mark McKeever, former Sheffield Wednesday and Northern Ireland international came in as a set piece specialist to relentlessly pick out centre back Holland who would finish with eleven league goals. Lewis Hogg, midfield dynamo, came in and would finish with thirteen yellow cards but was the penultimate piece in the jigsaw. The signing of Darren Edwards in the autumn was the ultimate one. City didn't exactly fly off the blocks, and I recall getting news of their home defeat by Stamford as I looked out on a grey September day in Luton little knowing what the future months would bring.

Most of us look back at the 1-0 away defeat at Hemel Hempstead as the pivotal moment. Certainly the team will remember the post game lock in from Relish as he asked serious questions about their desire and commitment. Three days later City thumped the now defunct Team Bath 5-0 and the die was cast. It set City on a run of 10 wins in 12 unbeaten games and clear top. A crucial three days saw a vital point at Kings Lynn and a win at Maidenhead. The 4-0 win at Hitchin at the end of March was evidence of the confidence that oozed through the team. It was also the last we would see of Scott Partridge that season as the footage of the game sees him troop off with what turned out to be a serious neck injury. When I see that clip now it is almost as if Scott has said 'My work here is complete', he had scored 18 goals that season. On and on City thundered cruising past Wealdstone when two successive draws had City fans worried. We had to go back to Northwood, where Wealdstone shared, a few weeks later, which meant going back to the pub with the exotic dancers. There are some things we miss about the Southern League. A Bank Holiday win over Chippenham in front of over 2,000 where signal problems in the streets of Manchester delayed hearing what was going on, and vital win over Maidenhead set up the final act. Or what we thought would be it.

Me and hundreds of City fans descended on Mangotsfield, near Bristol, increasing their gate five fold to over 1,000 on a Tuesday evening. A win would do as Team Bath were relentless in their pursuit. A draw was the outcome as we huffed and puffed and had two disallowed goals. So it was off to Yate four days later, again near Bristol (I was a fixture on the M4 around this time!) and increase their crowd by a factor of seven. An early goal down we had visions of having to win our final game the following Saturday to win the damn title. Not to worry. As all title winning teams do, at the moment when all around are losing their heads, strong men step forward. A corner, a header from Steve Jones brought us level, and then a marvellous piece of improvisation from Craig Davidge, one who polarises opinion but who will forever be the one who clinched the title. Final whistle and cue pitch invasion. Me, others, and my son who I had taken for this occasion, as my father had taken me to Leamington 29 years earlier.

And so to Conference South. Four wins in the first five games had us flying and top. While sustaining a place in the top six for a long time, a poor run in March left us relying on others and we finished 8th. An unbelievably hard FA Cup draw saw us win at new money Truro, old rivals Newport, and eventually lose to Conference side Torquay. The returning Dave Gilroy ably replaced Partridge and the season ended with the Somerset Cup win and Martin Paul overtaking Paul Randall as City's second all time scorer. The following season saw us recover from a dreadful start to gradually inch our way up the League until a calamitous FA Cup defeat at home to lowly Aylesbury United saw us lose £000s in prize money and a manager as John Relish decided to call it a day. Adie Britton stepped up to the plate knowing that we were now short of funds to bolster a promotion push. With Gilroy, Edwards and Douglas all chipping in City rose again only for a bizarre sequence of games saw three successive 1-0 defeats against lowly opposition followed by three wins - including a Stuart Douglas hat trick in a 4-0 win at Newport, his finest hour in a City shirt. It was all too late as City again finished 8th.

2009/10 dawned as Adie Britton's first full season and he had some immediate changes to make. Talismanic keeper Paul Evans had finally called it a day, replaced by Ryan Robinson, Sido Jombarti joined from Basingstoke, and forward Kaid Mohammed picked up after being released by Forest Green Rovers. All would play their part in what would be a truly momentous season. After an incredible opening game at

Chelmsford where City were 4-0 down in the first-half facing a penalty they recovered to lose 3-4 with ten men. Their next trip to Chelmsford would be far more profitable. City recovered then stuttered to be in the lower half of the division as their FA Cup campaign got underway with a couple of straightforward wins over lower league opposition and then a win over Totton in the final qualifying round. The prize? Away to Grimsby. At first glance not the plum we were looking for. Even looking at it several times you couldn't escape the fact that this was a 'Mansfield' of a draw. There were however a couple of differences this time. Grimsby were struggling at the bottom end of League 2 and City had found a bit of confidence and form. So in early November hundreds of City fans trekked to Cleethorpes, where Grimsby play, by coach, train, and car (thanks Kentish Tim). One of those had to be there days. We won 2-0 with a trademark Chris Holland header and a Darren Edwards turn and shot. We were well worth it and it could have been more. Grimsby fans were generous in their praise and we watched the ITV highlights later, and again and again and again. The Second round paired with Forest Green at home, a great chance to get to the Thirdround and our date at Old Trafford. However, City doesn't often convert great chances, and in front of over 3,300 for this all non-league tie we didn't. A Lewis Hogg equaliser, an untimely half time break and a sloppy second-half start were the ingredients and we were out. But we were richer, and this turned out to be the key to the other momentous part of the season.

Having savoured Cup success and long realised that good fortune to City fans might come now and again but certainly not twice in the same season, the team quietly went about its business, put together a nine game unbeaten streak in February and March to climb to third place. Newport was home and hosed as champions, but the play-off places were definitely up for grabs. Inevitable hiccoughs at Hampton and Basingstoke were more than made up for by a five game winning streak that saw them get fourth place in the play-off mix. I will always be glad that we didn't come up against Dover in the play-offs anywhere as I think they might have found us out. However, we found out Chelmsford 2-0 at home and an easier 1-0 away to set up a meeting with fifth-placed Woking at Twerton Park, home because we finished higher than them.

I think the play-offs have been good for football, but they haven't moved on. Rugby League has blazed the way, firstly with introducing them, and then by adapting them to ensure that higher place opposition get more of an advantage. In football having the second leg at home is just not enough. Ask Chelmsford and Dover. We had beaten Woking home and away quite easily, so City fans were rightly worried! To do it again would surely be against the odds. But it wasn't, we did, a Mohammed penalty in the second-half in front of almost 5,000 fans, the biggest gate at Twerton for almost fifteen years, brought City back to the non-league big time after thirteen years, and me back out on the Twerton Park pitch for the first time since that relegation to witness the trophy presentation and celebrations.

I finish this chapter quite appropriately in Luton, not only where I live but where City have just played. Three relegations since 2007 for the Hatters and two promotions for City have brought them amazingly, incredibly into the same division. Living in Luton for so long I have been to Kenilworth Road and Wembley to support them, but it was to the away end I ventured with 165 other City fans to cheer on our band of brothers into the next episode of this love affair. Passionate, loyal, maddeningly frustrating, totally illogical, but always inseparable. City til I die.

Dedicated to my Dad, Frank Dolan.

12

Arsenal

From Radford to Fabregas via Adams: Forty Years as an Arsenal Fan

Gary Sheffield

Arsenal Football Club seized hold of my emotions when I was a child and has stubbornly refused to let go. In fact, it has got worse. In my late forties I look back on many of my youthful enthusiasms with a sense of regret. As my career has advanced and I have become busier, I find it increasingly difficult to make time to do some of the things that I enjoy. And, to be frank, the gilt has worn off of some of them. If anyone asked me who my favourite singer was I would say, without hesitation, Bob Dylan. I discovered his music at the age of 18 and I have more of his albums loaded on my iPod than anyone else's. CDs. Listening to, say, *Blood in the Tracks,* I still love the richness of his language, the 'wild mercury sound', the harmonica, and above all that voice – the way he sings '*Bloooooooooooooooo*' on the last verse of 'Tangled Up in Blue' - sent shivers down my spine the first time I heard it, and still does. Dylan has provided the soundtrack of my adult life, the background music to my interior monologue. But. There is a big but. I have dutifully bought his recent CDs and listened to them on and off but with the exception of the odd track have thought them OK but nothing special. There. I've said it. I feel better now.

Not so with The Arsenal, as I learned to call them at an early age. I am more passionate about the team now than ever. Weekends can be made or blighted by the result of a game. If we have lost (I see that I have just written 'we' when I mean Arsenal) the feeling usually doesn't wear off until the next time we win. (We lost on Sunday, and it hurts). It really matters to me whether Ces Fabregas stays in North London or goes back to Barcelona. Ashley Cole went from hero to the opposite in my eyes because of his defection to Chelsea. And yes, I know that Sol Campbell's treatment of Tottenham in joining Arsenal was similar to Cole's. I just don't care – I was glad to have Sol back last season and wish him well at Newcastle. As I hinted earlier, logic simply doesn't enter it.

My advanced Arsenalmania has grown worse, in part thanks to 24/7 media and modern communications; I have more opportunities to feed my fanaticism than ever before. Only a couple of years ago I can remember being away from home one evening in a room without television or the Internet and having to wait, fingers crossed, for the Radio Five Live news to hear the result of a Champions League match. Then I acquired an iPhone... which has, quite apart from the Official Arsenal App, various ways of following a game live (I tend to flip between Sky Sports and the BBC. Being of that generation who experienced the Second World War second-hand through parents and grandparents, I still automatically regard the BBC as being authoritative, no matter what evidence might point in the other direction). Following the Gunners on my phone via updates from Caroline Cheese on the BBC website is just the latest, most technologically advanced way of being a football supporter. Because I rarely get to see the team play live.

In this, of course, I am scarcely unusual. Even the biggest club stadia, like the Emirates or Old Trafford, only holds about 60,000- 75,000 spectators. Arsenal's previous home at Highbury had a capacity roughly half of the new one. It is very difficult, if not impossible, to get tickets if you are not a season ticket holder, and not easy to become one. Add that to the fact that many fans, like me, live at a distance from the ground, or, also like me, often have to work on Saturdays (although teaching an MA course on the First World War is not exactly the equivalent of doing a shift down a coalmine). It follows that there must be many more fans of the biggest clubs who primarily follow their team via television, the Internet, and radio than ever sit in the stands.

Perhaps for us 'distance' fans the tension is greater than those who get to see the team play live week in, week out. Several years ago I took my son James to his first ever game at the Emirates, only to see Arsenal lose against West Ham (we had about 150 shots at goal and none went in – they had one and scored with it. The Hammers' keeper played a blinder, and I didn't blame him for running to the away fans at the end and throwing his gloves into the crowd. Name of Rob Green. What went wrong in South Africa against the USA?). The following season we saw Aston Villa win 2-0 at the Emirates. It was disappointing on both occasions, but least I got to see the team play and experienced the big match atmosphere. I'm sure I would have felt much worse had I been listening at home on Five Live. Or is that just the reaction of a country cousin up in the Big City for the day? Anyway, the fact that I get to see Arsenal play live but rarely has not lessened my devotion to the team. Writing this essay has made me analyse my devotion, and assess how it has become such a part of my identity.

My earliest football memory actually has nothing to do with Arsenal, and I can not only precisely date it but also time it to within half an hour. The date was 30 July 1966, and the time was around 5pm; the event was, of course the World Cup Final in which England played West Germany, still the England team's finest hour. Of the actual match I can remember precisely nothing. I had celebrated my fifth birthday a week before (by one of those curious tricks of memory, I can't remember my birthday but I can remember being excited about it the day before, playing on Clapham Common with my Dad), and if I had started watching the game on television - which like everyone else's in those days was a black and white set – I had given it up. What I can remember is kicking a ball in the hallway of our house, near the front door, wanting my Dad to come out and play football in the garden. He, poor man, was trying to explain about extra time.

This memory came back vividly 28 years later, in 1994, when I was trying to watch the FA Cup Final on television (Manchester United 4 Chelsea 0) and entertain my three-year-old daughter at the same time. I succeeded by telling her that her playgroup helper, a Man Utd fan, was at the game (true) and I had just spotted her in the crowd and we might see her again (most definitely false). It was enough to keep Jennie watching for a bit – that and encouraging her to shout 'Ooh, ah Canton-a' – the wayward French genius scored two penalties. She had been taught this at her playgroup and I was annoyed at the time because I didn't want her to be brainwashed into becoming a Manc fan. I needn't have worried. When Eric Cantona carried out his kung fu kick on a Crystal Place fan the following season, I encouraged her to be disgusted and that terrible fate was averted – although, sadly, now she doesn't follow football at all.

But I digress. The 1966 World Cup Final was a false start – my passion for the Arsenal began four years later, at some point between 15 March 1969 and 30 March 1970. The former was the date of the 1969 League Cup Final, when Arsenal lost at Wembley to then Third Division Swindon. This made absolutely no impact on me at the time, although it certainly did when I began to support Arsenal a short while latter. Even now, although we now live not far from Swindon and I sometimes watch local teams play, I haven't been tempted to spend a Saturday afternoon there.

The second date was when Arsenal played Crystal Palace and won 2-0. It was at Highbury, some 35,000 spectators attended and Dad and I were two of them. I'm pretty sure that the bug had bitten before the previous Christmas, as I remember wearing to the match an Arsenal hat, a sort of plastic baseball cap before such things were fashionable. I had already customised it before the game by writing 'Up the Gunners' on the peak, so can only imagine it had been a Christmas present.

Whenever precisely I fell for Arsenal – and the love affair has now lasted for over forty years - the immediate cause was parental influence. When I talk to people about the fact I support Arsenal (for some reason I have never been comfortable with calling myself a Gooner) I sometimes find myself being defensive for the simple reason that I would hate anyone to think that I was a Johnnie-come-lately who supports a big club because they are a big club. The jokes about Manchester United fans who live in Tunbridge Wells have a ring of truth about them. The purist in me says that there are only two valid reasons to support a football club: they are your local team; or your dad supported them. Under pressure I would admit that that there might be other acceptable circumstances, like other forms of local connections. In my case, Dad is from North London and is a life-long Gunners fan. Enough said, even though I was born and lived for the first 18 years of my life in South London, in the Wimbledon area. The majority of my school friends supported Chelsea, the nearest First Division team and a power in the land in the early 1970s, although I can remember a Fulham fan and some who followed Wimbledon, at that stage still in the Southern League. I can only recall one other Arsenal supporter in the school. I've often joked that as a Gunners fan growing up in a Chelsea supporting area I know what it is to be a persecuted minority.

My Dad's memories of Arsenal went back to when he was a kid in Forties, and I grew up on stories of the successful side of the immediate post-war era and the early Fifties. Arsenal had won the League Championship in 1947–48 and 1952–53, and the FA Cup in 1950 (and were beaten finalists in 1952). I was familiar with names like George Swindin, the goalkeeper; Jimmy Logie, the Scots inside forward; left half Joe Mercer, who in any case was a successful and popular manager of Manchester City (and briefly caretaker manager of England) in the late Sixties and early Seventies. I suppose that with this going on in the background, I stood no chance. My maternal grandfather used to tell me stories of the great days of Dulwich Hamlet between the wars, but although I was close to Grandpa, Arsenal won hands down.

I was aware of the wonderful heritage of the club. One boy at school used to irritate me intensely by saying 'lucky Arsenal' whenever we won. I knew – because I was the sort of kid to go away and read histories of football, even at the age of nine or ten – that this was a tag applied to Herbert Chapman's great Arsenal side of the Thirties, when they would defend and grab goals on the break. It was called *tactics*. As an historian, my spiritual home is the Britain of the pre-Thatcher twentieth century – dole queues, world wars, and rationing not withstanding. For almost as long as I can remember I have been fascinated by the history of the period just before my time, and reading of the period when Arsenal dominated the English game fitted in neatly with this. So at the age of nine I knew about Charles Buchan, Cliff Bastin, and Alex James with his baggy shorts. Ted Drake, I read, had had scored all seven in a 7-1 thrashing of Aston Villa in 1935. I took great pride in the fact that Arsenal won the League title three years on the trot in the 1930s, and winced at the fact that the only time the FA Cup has gone outside England was in 1927 when Arsenal's (ironically Welsh) keeper Dan Lewis fumbled the ball into the net gifting Cardiff City a 1-0 victory. Arsenal was a club with a great and glorious history, epitomised by the marble halls of Highbury. The nine year old me, even then a budding historian, rejoiced in it all.

What I did not know very much about was the Arsenal team of the Sixties. English football may have prospered during that decade, with European trophies going to West Ham (Cup Winners' Cup, 1965) and Manchester United (European Cup, 1968), and of course England's triumph over West Germany in 1966, but Arsenal hadn't. I avidly followed the 1970 World Cup in Mexico, including the build up, during which I read about 1966 and all that – and was disappointed to find not a single Arsenal player had made the squad, let alone played in the final. In truth, the period since Arsenal's League Championship win in 1953 had been a fallow time. They hadn't won a single trophy since, and although they had had some decent players like George Eastham and Joe Baker, they were pushed out of the limelight by teams like Manchester United, Manchester City, Liverpool and of course, our great rivals Tottenham Hotspur, who had won the League and Cup double in 1961, the year of my birth. There were signs of revival in the late Sixties, as Arsenal reached two successive League Cup finals in 1968 and 1969, only to lose both, to Leeds United, and Swindon Town. I have already referred to the humiliation of the latter occasion. But the year that I began supporting Arsenal marked the turning point – pure coincidence I am almost sure.

On Easter Monday, 30 March 1970, Dad and I set out from Garth Close, in the London suburbs but technically in Surrey, took the bus to Morden, the end of the Northern Line, and then the tube to Finsbury Park. We were going to see my first match. I was a little disappointed that we didn't go to Arsenal station – the only tube station named after a football team, as Herbert Chapman had persuaded the authorities to change the name of the station in the Thirties - but we first had to go to the house of someone he worked with, who lived very close to the ground and was (of course) an Arsenal fan.

Walking to the stadium, I can still recall the growing sense of excitement as we passed programme sellers, hotdog stalls and joined the throng of men and boys wearing Arsenal scarves and rosettes (Dad bought me a rosette). We queued to get into the West Stand – this was posh stuff; it cost 12/- for a seat as opposed to whatever it was to stand on the terraces of the North Bank. My first reaction to glimpsing the pitch was to marvel at how green it was. The second was to metaphorically pinch myself to see if it was actually true, that I was really there. In 2007, when I first went to the Emirates Stadium after a long period of not having seen Arsenal play live at all, at forty-something I had much the same reaction as I had had at the age of not yet nine. Being part of the crowd on match days has never lost its magic. Travelling across London on the tube, gradually more and more red and white scarves appear until getting out at Arsenal station you are caught up in a sea of fans. Reversing the journey, the scarves become fewer and fewer until getting on the train at Paddington you see a number of fans of other London clubs travelling west – and more often than not end up talking to a fan of a rival London team that was also playing at home that weekend.

Crystal Palace was not one of our big rivals but they were of course another London team, which gave the match a certain edge. I vividly remember a man in a nearby seat who was obviously dying to swear but in deference to the presence of children confined his shouts to things like "Palace pigs!" Arsenal ran out 2-0 winners. Nick, an old school friend and a Chelsea season ticket holder, recently related to me the devastating impact of seeing as a child his first ever match at Stamford Bridge - only to see his team lose. I was spared that.

That day against Palace the goals came from striker John Radford (a particular hero of mine) and the charismatic Charlie George. This was just a few weeks before Arsenal won its first European trophy, or indeed its first cup of any kind since that League Championship in 1953, and I was privileged to see the core of the successful 1970 side play.

In goal was Chesterfield-born Bob Wilson, who was later capped for Scotland when the rules were changed to allow players to appear for the country of their parents' birth, but at this match he was serenaded with chants of 'Wilson for England'. Sadly, with three keepers of the stature of Gordon Banks, Peter Bonetti and Alex Stepney in the England squad it never happened. The full backs were Pat Rice, an Arsenal legend, who later became club captain and who today is Arsène Wenger's assistant manager; and Sammy Nelson, Bob McNab's deputy who established himself as first choice later in the 1970s. In defence alongside Eddie Kelly and hard man Peter Simpson was Frank McLintock, the club captain. Big Frank, a Scotsman, was the beating heart of the team – a rugged man who seemed to me to be much older than the rest of the players on the pitch (in fact he was only 30 years old). Then there was Peter Marinello, a young, long-haired Scots 'new George Best' that Arsenal had bought for £100,000, a club record. Sadly, he could not cope with the pressure and crashed and burned. Next came Jon Sammels, an Arsenal mainstay who was to lose his place as a first team regular in the next season – I always thought him rather underrated; John Radford and Charlie George; and finally George Graham, later to be a successful if controversial manager of Arsenal from the mid-1980s to the mid-1990s.

At this point I have to admit my memory lets me down. Arsenal won the 1970 Inter-City Fairs Cup, the forerunner to the Uefa Cup (now recast as the Europa League) beating Anderlecht of Belgium 4-3 on aggregate over a two-legged tie. I cannot remember whether it was televised, or, if it was whether I watched it (I was not yet nine years old, remember). I can't even remember if it was on the radio. All I remember is having a deep sense of pride and excitement when I went to school the day after Arsenal had overturned Anderlecht's 3-1 advantage from the first leg by winning 3-0 at Highbury. I suppose I must have been disappointed by the result of the first leg, although the joy of victory drove that from my mind. At the end of my first season as an Arsenal fan we had won a significant trophy. It set high standards for the seasons ahead. I remember reading a football annual, presumably given as a present for Christmas 1970, which alongside an account of the epic, replayed 1970 FA Cup Final (Chelsea vs. Leeds – I supported the London team out of regional loyalty) had a piece on the Fairs Cup victory which ended with something like 'Well done Arsenal'. My heart swelled with pride.

It was to be over a year before I saw another match at Highbury, but it was worth the wait. On Saturday 17 April 1971, Arsenal played Newcastle United. We were chasing the Double of League Championship and FA Cup. Only one team had achieved this in the twentieth century: Spurs, ten years before. The team I saw play that day was the one that started the FA Cup final against Liverpool a month or so later: Wilson, Rice, McNab, Storey, McClintock, Simpson, Armstrong, Graham, Radford, Kennedy, George. I was pleased to see Bob McNab play. I had been desperately disappointed when, after being called up into the provisional England squad for the 1970 World Cup, he was one of six players sent home when the final 22 was announced. (Perhaps England World Cup managers have it in for Arsenal players. Out of four players axed by Bobby Robson from the preliminary squad for the 1990 World Cup, three – Tony Adams, David Rocastle and Alan Smith – played for the Gunners. However, in my 30th year, and shortly to become a father for the first time, I was not as nearly as devastated as I had been in 1970. In fact I had forgotten all about it until I read about very recently).

'Geordie' Armstrong, a brilliant winger, was another hero: I have a memory of him hurrying over to take a corner that April Saturday in 1971, soaking wet from the pouring rain. Above all, I remember the frustration of the Arsenal crowd, as the game ticked on and the score remained stubbornly at 0-0. The chant of 'give us a goal' to the tune of John Lennon's 'Give Peace a Chance' echoed around Highbury when Charlie George did just that, belting the ball through a congested penalty area with nineteen minutes left. The song then switched to 'Char-lie, Char-lie... born is the k-ing of High-bur-y' to the tune of the *First Noel.* We had no problems with One-Nil to the Arsenal that day.

The Palace match a year earlier had meant little in terms of the First Division. Arsenal had no chance of catching the leaders with only four league games to play. Eventually they finished 12th. Charlie George's goal against Newcastle, by contrast, kept Arsenal very much in the title hunt, especially because our rivals, Don Revie's Leeds United, lost to West Bromwich Albion that day. Walking away from Highbury in the pouring rain I was aware of an excitement, a buzz, that we were still in the race. I was aware of being a member of a community, along with my Dad; his friend (nicknamed 'Shiner' because he had a sideline in window cleaning), and the other 30,000 or so Gunners fans streaming away from the ground. It was a marvellous feeling that I have never forgotten. It got even better watching the game on *Match of the Day*, which I remember a lot less clearly than the controversial goal that West Brom scored against Leeds, and the 'sick as a parrot' whinging that followed. I have always thought that it was poetic justice, given that many Arsenal fans were convinced that Jack Charlton's goal ten days later that condemned the Gunners to 1-0 defeat was blatantly offside. Arsenal wrapped up the League title by beating Spurs, of all teams, at White Hart Lane. Ray Kennedy scored the only goal of the game, and it is nice to read that the Spurs manager, the legendary Bill Nicholson, sent champagne into the Arsenal dressing room.

The Spurs match wasn't televised, but the FA Cup Final of course was. Arsenal played Liverpool on 8 May 1971, and I watched all the build up on the television followed by the game itself. 0-0 at 90 minutes, Liverpool's Steve Heighway scored a few minutes into the first period of extra time. I can vividly remember Dad saying "Never mind, we've got the League", but of course George Graham equalised (although ultimately the goal was credited to substitute Eddie Kelly – but that is still a matter of controversy) and then Charlie George got the winner – a screaming 20 yard effort that ended with him flat on his back celebrating with his arms in the air. He had won Arsenal the Cup, and the Gunners had won the Double.

What did I feel? Excitement, jubilation, deep satisfaction: - all of the above. It was especially satisfying, and not only because the victory happened in my first full season as an Arsenal fan. It was the coming from behind that made it special. I felt the same feeling eight years later, when watching Arsenal on the TV beat Manchester United 3-2 in the 1979 Cup Final. Arsenal seemed to be breezing to a comfortable 2-0 victory when they conceded two late goals, which prompted disbelief mingled with despair. Then Alan Sunderland scored the winner – more disbelief, although this time of the good kind.

Ten years later it happened again at the end of what is surely the most extraordinary Arsenal game of all time. It took place on 26 May 1989, it was the last match of the League season, and Arsenal had to beat Liverpool by two clear goals at Anfield to seal the League Championship. Otherwise, Liverpool would add the League title to the FA Cup they had already won.

The match was televised, but out of a mixture of cowardice – I didn't want to see Arsenal fail – and pragmatism – I had some work to do– I left the TV to my wife that evening, and contented myself with switching on the radio at periodic intervals to find out the score. Nil-nil at half-time, Arsenal scored on 52 minutes, but one goal was not enough. As the match wore on, and my turning on the radio became more and more frequent, the more my conviction grew that this just wasn't going to be our year. When I finally left the radio on, about five minutes before the 90 were up, I just knew it wasn't going to happen. Then Alan Smith set Michael Thomas free with a wonderful pass, Thomas ran into the Liverpool box, and seconds later he had scored - 2-0.

The Arsenal fans up in Liverpool went mad. So did I. Roaring with delight, I went racing down the stairs into the sitting room, changed the television channel (to the bewildered protests of my long-suffering wife, brutally silencing *Inspector Morse* or whatever she was watching), and caught the very end of the match on the screen. Then the whistle went and Arsenal had won the League for the first time since the Double year of 1971. It was 1971 and 1979 all over again. If anything, it was even better.

Compared to most teams in the Football League, Arsenal had done well since 1971. Arsenal won the FA Cup in 1979, and the League Cup in 1987, but we had developed an unfortunate habit of being runner up – in the League in 1973, the FA Cup in 1972, 1978 and 1980, and in the European Cup Winners Cup in 1980 (I watched both of our 1980 Cup Final losses in the crowded common room of Barbier House, Bodington Hall, a University of Leeds Hall of Residence – which did not make defeat any easier to take, you can be sure). I had almost reached that point at which I was beginning to wonder if we would ever be good enough to win the title again (I seem to remember, Nick Hornby, author of *Fever Pitch*, the classic account of being an Arsenal fan in this period, was having similar doubts). Although beating Liverpool 2-1 in the 1987 League Cup Final was gratifying, 1989 restored my faith.

Managed now by George Graham –'Stroller' Graham of the 1971 Double-winning side – Arsenal were launched on their best spell since the 1930s. Another League Championship followed in 1991, the League Cup and FA Cup double in 1993 (not as good as the 'real' double but pretty satisfying nonetheless); and the European Cup Winner's Cup in 1994). George Graham's achievement has been overshadowed by what came after, yet he was the manager who instilled 'the habit of victory', to quote the title of a recent book on the history of the Royal Navy. Re-reading the excellent *Official History – Arsenal* by Phil Soar and Martin Tyler, I was reminded how dire some Arsenal seasons were in the 1970s and 1980s: 16th in the First Division in 1974-75; 17th in the following year; 10th in 1982-83. Arsenal never stood a real chance of becoming champions and we got used to this superior mediocrity (unfair I know, given our cup record). Today, in 2010, after five years without a trophy, in spite of top four finishes and reaching the 2006 European Champions League final, it *hurts*. All this is relative, of course. To finish 17th in the senior division of English football is beyond the wildest dreams of the vast majority of clubs. But we Arsenal fans have come to expect that as an absolute minimum we run the Premiership Champions close and qualify for the Champions League. This was not always the case. We have George Graham to thank for this.

When the Graham era ended, after a season's interregnum under Bruce Rioch – very much a forgotten man in Arsenal history - Arsène Wenger became manager in 1996. At the time I was working overseas at the University of Southern Mississippi, having carried out a job swap for six months. Speaking to my parents on the phone, Dad told me about Bruce Rioch's departure but the only things he could say about the new manager was that he was French, had been managing in Japan and his name sounded like Arsenal. That's about as much as any of us knew. In short order we discovered we had a *bona fide* footballing genius on our hands. Not only did he transform Arsenal, arguably he transformed English football.

1996 was for me, the pre-Internet age – it existed but I didn't have easy access to it and I didn't really know how to use it. Thankfully, one of my grad students at USM was a Brit (a Liverpool fan) who was IT literate and would tell me the weekend results on the Monday if I had missed them. Like many a Brit abroad, I grew to rely on the BBC World Service. I discovered that given the time difference, if I had a lie-in on a Saturday morning I could listen to the second half commentary of a match from my bed. This was the ultimate luxury – not that with two small children it was one I could indulge very often. I certainly listened to at least one Arsenal game on the

World Service (not from a prone position I think), a 2-1 defeat away to Nottingham Forest. I would buy the weekly *Guardian* and read the football reports, and make a regular trip to the University library where they had some British papers, a week or so old.

Wenger's management not only revolutionised Arsenal, but also what it meant to be an Arsenal fan. For years we had to put up with 'Boring Arsenal' and 'Lucky Arsenal' (and worse), and suddenly he created a highly attractive team that became a by-word for silky skills. The (second) Double-winning side of 1998 is still, I think, the Arsenal team that on purely aesthetic terms gave me most pleasure to watch. Alongside the likes of Dennis Bergkamp, Emmanuel Petit and Marc Overmars were the solid English qualities of Tony Adams (one of my all-time favourite players), Lee Dixon and David Seaman (one of a line of great Arsenal goalkeepers). Living in the shadow of Sir Alex Ferguson's Manchester United was tough, but when Arsenal came top – as in the Double years of 1998 and 2002, and winning the Premiership without losing a game in 2003-4 – they did so in style.

Arsène Wenger is a genius. Let no one be in any doubt about that. I just wish he'd buy to strengthen the squad. While favouring youth and not wishing to load the club with debt are of course laudable, in recent years we have been very unlucky with injuries – Fabregas, van Persie, Walcott, Gibbs and Eduardo to name but a few, and we simply haven't had sufficient depth in the squad to compensate. And take domestic cup competitions more seriously. I was not the only frustrated Gunners fan when a weakened Arsenal team was defeated by Stoke in the Fourth Round of the FA Cup in 2010. Interestingly, this 2010-11 season, perhaps at last appreciating the hunger of the Arsenal faithful for silverware, Wenger has put out teams in the Carling Cup that are much stronger than in the past. As a veteran Arsenal fan said to me recently, 'even the Mickey Mouse cup would be something'.

Arsenal teams in recent years have played some pretty football but all too often have lacked the killer touch, sometimes apparently trying to pass the ball into the net. I watched Arsenal play Birmingham City at the Emirates in 2007 with a couple of Blues fans. They marvelled at the sheer skill and artistry of the Arsenal players, and beforehand they were nervously wondering how big the Gunners' goal tally was going to be. Once the game had kicked off Arsenal's over-elaborate play contributed to their failure to put the game beyond reach when they were 1-0 up – and Birmingham went on to equalise and held on for a 1-1 draw.

The fact that a middle-aged man with no footballing talent whatsoever, someone who has a job in a completely different sphere, should feel the need to put on paper his criticism of one of the most successful managers in the history of British football speaks volumes about being a football fan. We care, passionately, about our clubs. It is part of our identity. As it happens, I have examined the concept of identity as part of my day job as a history professor, and as a consequence have thought about my own. People can (and usually) do have multiple facets to their identities. I am both an Englishman and a Briton. I am a husband and a father. I am a Christian and an Anglican (and as the Church of England is, quite literally, very broad, the exact shade of my Anglicanism could be further defined). I am an academic military historian, with varying levels of allegiance to the institutions where I was educated and employed. And I am an Arsenal fan.

Although I get to see the team play live all too rarely, I feel part of a community. I follow Arsenal on the television, newspapers and Internet. I am nervous when they are playing, downcast when they lose, happy when they win, ecstatic when they win trophies. If I had to choose between England winning the World Cup or Arsenal winning the Champions League, club would trump country every time. That my son enjoys watching Arsenal is a source of satisfaction. My nephew Jack is following in the family tradition by supporting the Gunners. It gave me great pleasure to take him to his first Arsenal game - unfortunately a 0-0 draw against Sunderland, but at least he saw Andrey Arshavin's first appearance. It also gave me great pleasure to take Dad to see his first game at Arsenal's new home at the Emirates – a hugely satisfying 4-1 thumping of Portsmouth in the first home game of the 2009-10 season. I've always enjoyed the gallows humour of football fans, and I'll never forget being in a crowded tube carriage hearing Pompey fans serenade us with "You only won four-one'.

When you meet a fellow Gunners supporter, you have something in common (actually, that is true when you meet a genuine fan of whatever club). And you find them all over the place. In 2007 I invited Professor Saul David to give a lecture at the University of Birmingham. At the time, we didn't know each other very well, but we had a congenial dinner at a restaurant afterwards. Every so often I would check my mobile phone (a very primitive affair) as my colleague Dr John Bourne, a Port Vale fan, was sending me texts updating the score of Arsenal's Champions League match. After a while Saul cautiously asked me if I was interested in the Arsenal game – and of course, it came out that he too was a Gunners fan. The conversation then took a very different turn...

In the end it is all about belonging. I enjoy watching football for its own sake if there is nothing at stake. I love watching my local team, Wantage Town, not least because I am pleased when they win, but not too bothered if they don't. Football with no pressure: it is different with the Arsenal.

I'll finish with my favourite ever Arsenal goal. It wasn't scored by the likes of Thierry Henry or Malcolm Macdonald, Robert Pires or David Platt, Alan Ball or Jack Wilshere. The goal I treasure most was scored by Tony Adams, Arsenal's captain and one of our greatest ever defenders. It came in May 1998, against Everton at Highbury in a match where a win would give us the Premiership title. I went to watch it in a pub near my then home in Camberley, Surrey. With a couple of minutes to go we were 3-0 up, and the atmosphere in the pub, let alone at Highbury, was fantastic. Then substitute Steve Bould put Tony Adams through. He chested it down, picked his spot, and stuck in the back of the net –'like a centre forward' as the television commentator said. It was a real captain's goal. Arsenal were Champions. It felt wonderful. Watching the clip on YouTube, it still does.

13

Sheffield United

*United Hates F****** Cockneys!*

Jack Simpson

Supporting a football team is like being wrongly convicted of a murder that you did not commit. On the one hand, it is a life sentence from birth to death, cradle to the grave, vagina to vegetation; on the other, it is inescapable, no matter how much you try and escape there is a set of virtual - in my case red and white - bars that hold you in. My sentence at birth was immediate and it was a lifetime of supporting Sheffield United. In itself this is not a unique feat, but when you consider I was born in the postcode SE14 (London) rather than S2 (Sheffield – beautiful downtown Bramall Lane), you can see the peculiarity of my twenty year relationship with the Red and White Wizaaaaaaaaaaaaaaaards.

Although not every second has been exactly magical, supporting Sheffield United has had its moments of wizardry. Three FA Cup Semi Finals, one League Cup Semi Final, three Play-off Finals and one promotion to the Premier League all in the space of my short lifetime. At first glance, this looks rather impressive and for many teams it would be. In fact, for a return on twenty years I appreciate that I can't complain…not like what older fans have been put through Robert Simpson. However, when you reverse the half full glass to half empty an alternative reality emerges. And it is here that there is a certain synergy with those older fans' experiences and the collective reality is more in tune with what being a Blade is all about…three play-off final defeats without scoring… without even turning up to be honest…on each occasion … one relegation with the last kick of the season to a team who rightfully should have been concentrating on their Cup final the following weekend… and another on the last day of the season with a penalty winner from a player we had sold for nothing just four months earlier ... and who had missed a penalty against Blackburn playing for the Blades earlier in the season that would have bagged the extra points for safety. Oh yes, I had forgotten to mention the two relegations...and we won't even mention the Don Givens contribution to United history as that is before my time and so out of the remit of this chapter strictly speaking (but the older fans I can see still weeping; well, according to my mother who swears that Dad was very 'upset').

But I am not bitter, I'm not really. As we all know, supporting a football team isn't merely just about success on the pitch it's about everything else that comes with it – the full Monty (incidentally what a player!) but in this case fully clothed. There is no doubt that disappointment and failure have been a significant factor in my growing up with the Blades. I've grown to appreciate how character forming football can be. Losing is just as much of a part of being a football fan as winning and when you experience both I feel your ying and yang become perfectly aligned. Being a Blade has given me that balance to my life that many other clubs would not provide. When life's a bit crappy there is nothing like a last minute winner against Leeds to pull you out of the doldrums. Equally, if life's great and nothing can knock me off my ninth cloud a 2-1 defeat to Wigan is the perfect way of the football gods taking the prayer mat from under my feet while pronouncing, 'That teaches you for getting above yourself, you self-congratulatory being'. If nothing else is consistent in my life, at least the Blades are always there and you know exactly what you will get from them. If Isaac Newton was a football fan he would be a Blade as he understood 'To every action there is always opposed an equal reaction: or, the mutual actions of two bodies upon each other are always equal, and directed to contrary parts'. In many ways this balance of success and failure has made me into the level headed sane guy I am today. For example, if I supported West Brom, I'd probably be bipolar; if I supported Arsenal I'd be a person of style but no substance and if I supported Bradford City I might be a twenty year old manic depressive – like a few I know. Thank goodness for the Blades

So I hear you cry 'Why Sheffield United?' This is a question I have regularly asked myself throughout most of my conscious life. How do I explain how I have ended up the way I have?

Glory Hunter! Could be one accusation. It is true that at the age of four I saw the bright lights of the Anglo Italian Cup and thought 'Yeah! I got to get me a piece of this action'. After all, why would you want to support a team that could be playing Barcelona at the Nou Camp in the Semi Final of the greatest football competition in the world, when you had the chance of seeing your team playing Ascoli in a competition that could only be described as a footballing version of Kevin Costner's 'Waterworld' - 'Yes it did actually happen and there's proof... but better off forgotten'. Although I have had my moments when supporting the Blades, I don't think anyone in their right mind would see me as a glory hunter.

For practical reasons maybe? It is true that if you step out of my house take the London Overground for ten minutes to London Bridge, wait for the irregular Saturday Northern Line service to St Pancras for another twenty-five minutes, get on the train up to Sheffield that only takes two hours during the week but closer to three on Saturdays, followed by a brisk walk of fifteen minutes, you are at Beautiful Down Town Bramall Lane (BDTBL) - a whole three hours and seven minutes. That's two hours forty-five minutes longer than it would take to get to the New Den or two hours fifteen minutes longer than it would take to get Selhurst Park and the Valley respectively or even, heaven forbid, two hours longer than it would take to get to Loftus Road. Alright, it isn't exactly on par with Carlisle nor Torquay but Bramall Lane isn't the most practical ground to get to from SE14.

So this leads to the only reason to me supporting Sheffield United Football Club and that is inheritance. There is a lot I have inherited from my dad since my arrival at Easter 1990 - dark hair, a slow turn of pace, a rather sizable head. However, the one feature that defines me most is that of the football team he passed on to me. From the day I was born, although I was not fully aware at the time, I was a Blade. I was to support

Sheffield United Football Club. It was destined...the life sentence began.

To the untrained eye I was very much a normal five year old that enjoyed five year old things, such as playing with toys, climbing trees and making girls cry. However, the fact I supported Sheffield United in many ways left me feeling isolated and at times very alone. When I look back, with the benefit of hindsight I can understand now why shoes that light up when you step or glow in the dark may have captured more interest in the school playground than a recount of the Blades game against Wolves the previous Saturday. While I was surrounded by Arsenal, Man United and Liverpool shirts there would not be a school picture or class performance where I wasn't wearing the two scimitars and white rose emblazoned on my chest. While playing the role of Fagin, I maintained the Red and White stripes under a long coat for the length of the play. As you have probably guessed, the production was neither geographically nor historically accurate. While my friends filled their heads with dreams of being their heroes like Alan Shearer or Thierry Henry, all I wanted was a picture of Bobby Ford. Unfortunately, I had to settle for Paul Gascoigne in a giveaway at my local football club. In hindsight, I would have preferred life imitating art as five or so seasons of watching Bobby Ford's mediocre left wing play would have had me giving my right arm to swap him for Gazza.

The difference between my peers and I, sufficed not only in social circles but even extended to my school work. I was by no means an underachiever but there was a common theme that ran throughout my essays and assignments. Each week in my formative years, we had to stand in front of the class and tell our classmates what we had got up to during the previous weekend. While others stood and recounted tales of their parents taking them swimming at Deptford Wavelengths or to a film at Peckham Multiplex or the odd lucky ones that were taken to Chessington World of Adventures, I had very different stories to recount. My reports contrasted with anything that went before as well as contrasting with anything

Social Services would have condoned. So when I was asked, 'So Jack what did you do this weekend then?' I was literal and graphic. 'Well miss, I went to Stoke-on-Trent'. 'And what did you do in Stoke-on-Trent?' while ironing out the quizzed look on her face. 'First of all we went to Macdonalds and I got to eat a giant big Mac, and then we went to the pub for two hours, then my dad let me have some of his pint and then we went to the football match; there was lots of big men there and they all kept on shouting stuff like 'shove that card up your arse referee' and 'What the f***…?'. 'That's quite enough Jack!' You can imagine how much my mimicking of those men caught on in the playground. You couldn't move for hearing 'go shove that card up your arse'. The phrase 'shove that card up your arse' became very popular in December when we were all swapping Christmas cards.

There is a blissful period in everyone's life, even the most pessimistic person's life (probably one of the blokes I sit next to at the Lane) where life is easy and the weight of the world is merely a pin prick on the clavicle. Ok I may come across a tad pretentious and as if my problems as a teenager were deeper than anyone can comprehend. However, if you've seen 'Skins' you will understand the troubles we go through, how serious they are and how the world just misunderstands us. My addiction to class As and white spirit is a direct result of my girlfriend of three days leaving me for a 40 year old father of six. But seriously it was easier then. 'Back when I was a lad' it was a choice between which Power Ranger you liked better Green or White (for those in the know you will realise these are the same person). Now we have to think about exams, jobs or which cider to go for - Frosty Jack's or Strongbow, a major problem when you only have £3.48 in your pocket. This early corridor in your life of emotional freedom leads to instances of losing at Street Fighter, getting told you weren't allowed to sit next to your friend on the carpet at school and most importantly Sheffield United's fortunes rise in prominence to fill the void that relationships, money and employment haven't yet polluted. The feelings of disappointment, frustration and depression never diminish but as you get older they are in a wider context of boring things such as responsibility.

My biggest feeling of the Bill Shanklyism 'football being far more important than life' came in the 1996/97 campaign. This was the first season where I truly knew I was a Blades supporter. By this point I hadn't experienced my fifteen years of 'so close, yet so far' and had this in-built belief that the story of Sheffield United was like a swashbuckling tale such as Robin Hood Prince of Thieves (it is mere coincidence I have referenced to Kevin Costner films in the first few pages...Do not worry it is not a theme) where we always beat the villain and got the girl.

To me the play-offs were like the exciting climax of any film or story. Finishing fifth and against all odds, we would somehow defeat all comers and reach the promised land - the Premier League. Imagine my excitement at the vindication of this hypothesis when we squeezed past Ipswich on away goals in the Semi-Final. At this age, it was only football that authorised any latitude with my sleeping hours and I remember being allowed to stay up and follow the conclusion of the match. This was about five years before any decision to update to Sky and the internet had not yet been installed in the Simpson household so teletext was the best way to keep abreast of events in Suffolk. So, crammed around our Panasonic my sister, brother and I were transfixed on the hypnotic, luminous letters – a sea of greens, blues, yellows and whites – that Ceefax conveyed its information through. My brother was on 'channel up/channel down' duty every minute and a half so that the page would refresh; in that way we made sure that no goal, sending off or penalty decision would be missed.

The game swayed from side to side with each team grabbing and losing the initiative. A goal by marksmen Petr Katchuro in the first five minutes sent United 2-1 up on aggregate but was cancelled out taking the tie to extra time. During extra time, it was Ipswich that seemed to be heading to the Prem after making it 3-2 on aggregate. However, when the name Walker appeared in green letters, we knew that we would be going through on away goals, a system which I found baffling at the time but now can clearly see its merits in this instance (although it was subsequently abandoned). For those who are experienced in the lost art of 'Ceefax-ing' the appearance of a goal always provides a sense of pulse-racing excitement; but when looking to hold onto a result, it is that all important red FT that becomes most wanted. Whereas with Gillette Soccer Saturday or Final Score today the result is produced on screen within seconds of the full time whistle being blown, on Ceefax there was always that dreaded longer wait. These extra minutes made it feel like hours and to a child of seven, it felt like days! It is as if the Ceefax god is a Wednesdayite leaving you in play-off final limbo. When the red FT finally did appear, we had done it and there were scenes of jubilation throughout South East London – well ok… in our front room. The Blades were going to Wembley, I was going to Wembley for the first time to see the Blades and as any Hollywood tale ends it would assuredly result in us being a Premier League team.

It must be said there is something magical walking down Wembley Way for any football fan. I feel this is heightened when it is a play-off final. It is unlike any other game in the country that can evoke such a range of various emotions. I was too young to fully realise at the time but arguably it is the biggest game of the season with the vast financial rewards at stake but more importantly, both sides have maximum attendance of the real fans. By the end of one set of ninety minutes, you can feel the jubilation of promotion and the prospect of mixing it with the big boys for a season. Conversely, you can find yourself dragging your body away from the twin towers, moping over the Cardiff moat or retreating from the Wembley Arch (I have experienced all three – I'm a Blade remember) with the cold comfort coming from the fact you will get another chance to visit the Priestfield stadium one more time the following season. You can feel the hope and expectation of nearly seventy thousand fans on both sides immersed in a carnival atmosphere. The colours are overwhelming, the sound is deafening and the smell of expectant perspiration – as well as inebriation - fill the nostrils. As a child, the whole occasion was quite foreign and this led to Chris, one of my dad's mates kids who was exactly my age at the time, bursting into tears (sorry about that Chris). Perhaps it was seeing the unity and happiness of so many people in such a confined space that triggered off his inner emotions and the result was tears of joy. Alternatively, it may have been that despite his tender years he was more wisened to the ways of Sheffield United and play-off finals and thought it was probably best to get his cry out of the way before the game. I suspect it was this innate seventh Blades' sense.

In many ways the 1996/97 play-off final was a battle of attrition for the players and a battle to keep awake for the fans. The play-off final finals are usually associated with amazing goals, nail biting drama and major incident. For the most part the 1996/97 play-off final was devoid of all of these things. However, there was a moment where an amazing goal, produced a moment of high drama and incidentally was with the last kick of the game. With the end of normal time coming to a close, a ginger haired Scotsman by the name of David Hopkin picked up the ball just outside the box and sent a looping shot that managed to curl perfectly in between post and bar to Simon Tracey's left hand side and nestled in the back of the Wembley net. That was it. I've never known a moment of finality like it. Hardly time to kick off again. Yes, if you haven't guessed yet, Hopkin was a Palace player and he had turned a seven year old optimist into a football realist... or more commonly known a 'Blade'. This was my coming of age in life and it appropriately took place at the age of seven.

Unfortunately, the David Hopkin experience also resulted in me being wary of ginger people. This is not because I dislike or have anything against people of a ginger persuasion. It is only because I am of the thinking that, as David Hopkin did to me at the age of seven, anything that I receive or take from a ginger person they in turn will remove or take back in the most heart breaking way. This even plagues me to this day. I am constantly living in fear that my student overdraft will be cancelled; the reason for this? The efficient, friendly and all round pleasant bank clerk Paul, is ginger. Some people have nightmares about falling from great heights, others are kept awake by thoughts of Michael Myers or being buried alive. My biggest fear is a ginger Scottish bloke in a Palace shirt coming into my bedroom at night, removing my heart and then expertly curling it with his right foot through the top right hand corner of my window. Irrational it may seem, but then this is what being a football fan is all about.

The torment of my first play-off final experience did not just stop with the hurt received from a last minute winner against my team. Unlike the sensible 'Unitedite' who made a swift getaway up the M1 or to St Pancras to the safe haven of the North, for some reason my ever optimistic dad had arranged to meet people in the Wembley car park for a sort of car boot pork pie/champagne reception. Well the champagne was kept on ice and the party atmosphere seemed absent. Being seven, I was far too young to drown my sorrows and I've never been much of a pork pie man. And so it was the party that never was and while they all spun away from the car park and headed off up north to join the M1 via the north circular we had to trudge down the Wembley Way accompanied by thousands of jubilant Palace fans who by now had done all the celebrations and were exiting the stadium; they were heading back south of the river in the same direction as the SE14 Blades.

Cup runs for teams in the Championship are to say the least unusual, two in a season nearly unheard of, two cup runs and a league campaign that led to United being just a game away from the Premier League well a bloody miracle. The 2002 season started with a disappointing but promising 2-1 defeat at Highfield Road but who was to know that it would end sixty plus games, thousands of accumulative miles on the road and zillions of goals later in Cardiff at the greatest anti climax to a football season in my history. From the New Den to Old Trafford the season had had it all - thrills, spills, massive successes and even greater disappointments. As with any great moment in history there are turning points and catalysts that make everything that eventually happens happen. Whether it was the Soviet Union's victory at Stalingrad or the misplaced match that triggered the Fire of London, our spark came on a November night at Bramall Lane – a Yorkshire derby between United and the hated Leeds. As usual they arrived full of swagger but this time it was to end in tears for the opposition.

As I have alluded to earlier as a football fan that has to go to school the next day and live where the stadium isn't a matter of a swift walk or a brief car journey, you have to make the most of alternative coverage of the Blades games. Unfortunately, being an armchair Sheffield United does not entail as much game viewing time as say an armchair Manchester United fan. Many an hour has been spent on the BBC website watching the amusingly brief and annoyingly concise minute by minute summaries or attempting to paint a mental image through the words of Jonathan Pearce.

Having listened to football on the radio for a number of years, there is always a pattern as to what happens when a goal is scored. In the case of Phil Jagielka's 30 yard spectacular equaliser it followed this pattern perfectly. 'Jagielka picks up the ball 30 yards out'. Pause. Commentator assesses situation and what Jagielka will do next. Listener is relaxed. Not too much sound coming from the crowd and 30 yards out that is not anything to get excited about…yet. 'HE SHOOTS'. Commentator is taken by surprise his utterance is brief and of a hurried nature. The surprise in the commentator's voice alerts the listener, he takes his gaze from where it was to the source of the noise, assumes a bent forward sitting position and grips the sofas arm rest a little tighter. SILENCE FROM COMMENTATOR. Listener holds breath. QUEUE INCOMPREHENSIBLE SOUND WITH RISING INTONATION. Listener stays silent, bends further forward in expectation of getting out of seat, still not fully aware that a goal has been scored waiting for the delayed sound of the crowd and the commentator to utter the words 'goal' or 'scored'. Sound of the crowd. 'IT'S IN. JAGIELKA HAS SCORED'. Two insurances that the goal is legally registered, green light for the proceeding chaos in the front room to begin. This feeling of ecstasy was only bettered two minutes later when with the last kick of the game Peter Ndlovu had scored the winner. Exit the hated Leeds. Radio would play a major part of this season for me so much so that we somehow ended up with a CD of the commentary of the two cup runs that we have subsequently downloaded onto my windows media player. It always takes me to a better place when a bit of John Mayer is abruptly followed by Toby Foster's on Radio Sheffield commentary on Michael Boulding's goal against Wycombe in one of the early rounds of the Carling Cup.

The biggest influence on my football knowledge, opinions and unfortunately loyalties has to be my Dad 'the football conspiracy theorist'. Like fundamental Christians in America indoctrinate rubbish such as 'God Hates Homosexuals' or are made to preach in mall car parks in places like Ohio. I was indoctrinated from an early age 'Arsenal were the enemy' and were told to preach the words of 'our father' (not the big man, but actually my dad) to anyone who was willing to listen. In secondary school before I knew any better I stood there programme in one hand forcing my point of view on the masses, which consisted of a few of my mates. Predictably, this conversion to my beliefs often failed. For the most part I was hit back with 'Yeah but Sheffield United are shit' this caused 'endgame' for my argument. How could I argue against something I knew to be inherently true?

I liken my Dad's relationship with Arsène Wenger to that of the relationship portrayed between Helga and Arnold in the popular 1990s cartoon 'Hey Arnold'. Like Helga, my dad is wracked with strong feelings (in this case of hatred) he feels towards Wenger and has to limit these outbursts to heart felt asides and delicately constructed scrapbooks dedicated to his nemesis. Conversely like Arnold; Wenger is blissfully unaware of my father's emotions directed towards him and let's be honest any knowledge of his existence.

It transpired recently while on holiday during a rummage through his wallet most likely to 'borrow some euros' for the night's festivities that his dislike for Arsenal and Arsène Wenger was so much that he had begun to build a case against his arch nemesis. I can hear it now in that standard cinematic trailer voice 'The story of one man and his fight against injustice….Coming to screens near you George Clooney plays Robert Simpson in…..The Ballad of a Twisted and Bitter Man'. A plastic wallet held together a collection of about ten different paper cuttings that spanned the previous six months. As I thumbed through there were various different headlines that covered topics such as Wenger's red card dynasty, Wenger's propensity to 'never see anything', Wenger's inability to field English players and Wenger's total lack of generosity in defeat. Apparently this was his evidence book whenever he put his case forward in the pub on the variety of Arsenal-related issues. In many ways, this is a more evidential but far less mature mirror of what I used to do in the playground at school and funnily enough the times I've been to the pub with my Dad his arguments are usually followed by a far more adult version of 'Yeah but Sheffield United are crap'. There is a recurring image that comes to me of my Dad locked away in his shed having some kind of 'Beautiful Mindesque' mental breakdown, surrounded by paper cuttings and being dragged by his feet shouting 'The Gooners, they're out to get me'. Although with regards to this there are many points I agree on with my Dad I cannot get as fanatical as him about it. It is almost Biblical in his beliefs and I'm talking first testament Biblical. To him there was a time when football was pure and righteous and everyone got along in a football Eden. However, when Arsène Wenger came to England a poison was spread and diving, blind managers and two footed challenges reached 'Fever Pitch' (No pun intended).

Promotion to the Premier League came with all the usual bonuses that one would associate with the situation. Trips to major grounds, being able to watch your team on Match of the Day and people no longer asking 'Who do you support again, Sheffield (wash out my mouth with soap and water) *Wednesday*'. However, there was an unpleasant anxiety that stuck with me from May and through the early weeks of August. This was a result of the impending certainty that I would have to manage and support a team that participated in the same league. Fantasy Football is one of those things that you can never really win anything from other than kudos but you find yourself watching 'Match of the Day' every week asking questions such as did the flick off Kevin Nolan's thigh count as an assist.

The mixture of management and emotions never merge well and by the first week of the season I had already made my first mistake. As the likes of Peter Taylor and Mark McGhee had done before me, I signed Ade Akinbiyi. It quickly became clear that Ade equalled Akin 'bad' biyi and he embodied a problem I would have throughout the season. How do I find the balance between my own interests and the interests of Neil Shipperley's Super XI. The game against Blackburn was a perfect example of this. While being a very sad day for me, as two penalty misses from Hulse and ironically David Unsworth, deprived us of our first league win of the season. With regards to my fantasy team (I would like to point out at this point the word fantasy and the fact it does not belong to reality shows how sad this paragraph makes me sound) Brad Friedel's clean sheet and two penalty saves did earn me a cheeky 22 points, unheard of for a goalkeeper. On the same line of thought, Reading a couple of weeks ago got me torn in two again. When two nil down Rob Hulse grabbed a goal back from a cross by Akinbiyi for us, this may have got us back into the game and provided us with the opportunity to gain a point. However, I couldn't help but think that Shorey's clean sheet had gone and why did I put Akinbiyi on the bench.

There was only one way around this I would have to separate my heart from my head and yes it did cause an emotional stroke at times but it was essential. My heart would have to go one hundred per cent with the Blades and my head had to go fully into the Fantasy team (more often than not against the blades). So when in mid-September, we played Arsenal I filled my team with Arsenal players. Gallas got a clean sheet and Fabregas bagged himself a couple of assists. With a performance bonus as well, twenty six points between them had me doing the inverse of R.Kelly when it comes to 'a little bit of bump and grinding'. My mind was telling me yes but my body....my body...was telling me Noooooo!'.

Being promoted with the likes of Paul Ifill and Chris Lucketti in your ranks there is certain inevitability about a relegation dogfight. As fans of West Ham and Liverpool will know at the moment, a good old season for survival means every point counts double and every win means that little bit more and getting anything from one of the top four is nigh on a miracle. Although, the end of the season result maybe wasn't what we had planned and maybe what we had deserved there were some great moments that came as a result.

The opening day of the season was in theory going to be the baptism of fire for us. Liverpool at home was going to be our lesson in what Premier League football was all about. As with any keen cricketer football takes a back seat from late April to the middle of May and August through to late September. Liverpool fell into this time bracket and an afternoon switching my attentions between what was going on in the middle and what was going on at the Lane. I was in fourth wicket down and being forty three for three left me standing between pavilion, dressing room and outside. While just passing through the threshold of the pavilion I heard that standard Sky Sports News phrase 'And we can tell you there has been a goal at Bramall Lane'. Bated breath. When the Sheffield United one Liverpool nil appeared in blue, red and white at the bottom of the screen I didn't wait for an explanation I just went running and screaming. Bat in one hand and helmet in the other all those out in the middle stopped to looked for a Budgie having an orgasm noise but instead saw me shaking and jumping manically. That day instead of it being a case of 'the rain stops play' it was more a case of 'deranged stops play'.

February the tenth marked the point of the season where we had made it to the magical thirty point mark, seven points clear of the drop and the performance of the season where I actually felt for the first time we belonged in the Premiership. Against a Tottenham side who boasted nine regular internationals and after going behind in the first five minutes eighty minutes of domination proceeded. With the very much Championship strikers Rob Hulse and Jonathan Stead, the Tottenham could not handle the aerial bombardment that was being handed to them. With a penalty from the Phil Jagielka being the decisive winning goal, the Blades in theory only needed another ten points from our last eleven games to 'be safe'. However, in the space of three weeks we had proceeded to lose two games with an aggregate score line of 11-1 and most importantly our player of the season and talisman Rob Hulse had broken his leg. Many look at the Tevez Affair as the central reason behind going down which is true but rivalling it to a great extent is the minute we lost Rob Hulse. Doesn't football have a way of biting you in the bottom?

As you may have become aware of throughout this chapter, as a South Londoner I have a very strong aversion to those Red and White pretentious continental group of players that are housed North of the Thames. Before all you Brentford or Leyton Orient fans start picking up your pens to write your letters of complaint, put them down, I am talking about Arsenal of course, you are not that important. Playing in Red and White is about the only thing we share in common with Arsenal. Where we play lovely fluid football *Cough Kevin Blackwell* and play football in the right spirit *Cough Chris Morgan*, Arsenal are a bunch of hackers that seem to cheat all the time. This made the victory against them in 2006 even sweeter. On a bitterly cold night just before New Year's Eve in Sheffield Neil Warnock did a Mick McCarthy on us and made eight changes or so to the starting line up. We had a little known about strikeforce of Colin Kazim-Richards and Christian Nade playing that night. Kazim played the ball towards Nade marshalled closely by Kolo Toure he then let the ball run through his legs, turned the Ivorian international while leaving him on his now rather cold backside and curled it past the onrushing Jens Lehmann.

After half time controversy and action was rife, it began with Morgan displaying on Van Persie's rib cage what he later nearly fatally perfected on Ian Hume and then twenty odd minutes of time left to play an injury to Paddy Kenny made it possible for Phil Jagielka to play in goal. With versatility being his middle name Phil Jagielka is one of the only players apart from maybe Alan Fettis where the chant 'England's Number One!' could be extended to 'Two…Three…Four…. Six and Eight' and still be half right. Having obviously been created by a Pole the wall in front of the home team's goal was unbreakable and we held on to win one nil. 2006 had ended with a bang but I don't think anyone could have predicted the fireworks that would erupt in 2007.

At this point you are probably expecting a couple of paragraphs on the whole Tevez affair but much ink and breathing time has been spent on this and all you want to hear now is an essay on why I think West Ham were wrong instead I will tell you what I did about it.

I've never been much of a politicised person. I keep abreast of what's going on loosely and watch 'Have I Got News For You' every week but that is about as far as my political fervour takes me. I have no French blood whatsoever and do not share that need to get off my arse and stand up for something I believe in. During the recent 'Students against Raising Fees Protest' the only draw for getting me down to London was the subsidised two pound bus I could get down there. I was thinking; hang around for twenty minutes slink off home and bang I have just saved myself the extra one pound fifty Megabus would have had me pay. In Secondary School, there was a group of my friends that decided to play truant and walk on Parliament with the likes of George Galloway in protest against the War in Iraq. I didn't really disagree that much with the war on Iraq and double games definitely clinched it for me. So what was I doing in the middle of June missing school, walking towards Parliament next to a seven foot pirate? I suppose if you were going to compare George Galloway and Captain Blade on political credibility George Galloway probably just edges out Captain Blade by a 'whisker'. Nevertheless, Captain Blade may prance about in front of twenty thousand people waving his Styrofoam swords on a Saturday but at least he has never pretended to be a thirsty cat eating out of the hands of a washed up actress in front of five million of the British public on live T.V.

The 'campaign for justice in football' was not exactly the 'storming of the Bastille', but the two coach loads of Unitedites, a few Sheffield United directors, Sean Bean and some bloke who used to be on The Bill had a goal and that was to be heard in the Houses of Parliament. Ok when I put it like that it may have been rather feeble in numbers nevertheless, what a great day. How many football fans do you know that have marched on Parliament for their team to maintain integrity in football. Integrity was not the word to describe the journey towards Westminster it was Sheffield United in theme and organisation, a bloody shambles. At the front you had 'Boromir' leading his Knights of Rotheram towards the gates of Mordor' chanting protest songs whilst slipping the 'Greasy Chip Buttie Song' in there somewhere. In between these there were your group of stragglers that obviously loved the experience of London far more than the actual march. In this group you had photographers taking pictures of the sights, window shoppers eyeing up the souvenir shop fronts all the while half chanting half not. Then at the back was 'Captain Blade' thriving in the attention he was getting from a group of Spanish schoolgirls that all wanted a picture with him. I've always wondered why at United games Captain Blade is assisted by a person not in a comical seven foot mascot suit. I now know he is the overseer making sure the Captain doesn't get too close to the Bladettes.

Getting into Parliament provided other obstacles mostly brought on by the Security team, I do worry for the safety of our country when half an hour is spent on making sure all those wearing Sheffield United shirts had their garments turned inside out. Following this debacle we got into the 'Home of Democracy'. It was a hilarious scene fifty or so Sheffield United fans being escorted through the extremely austere interior in our synthetic inside out football shirts. We were taken into the Palmerston Room and then sat through what was well meant but not the most enthralling session of speeches and questions and answers. I clapped in all the right places and didn't yawn too loudly. Then it came for Sean Bean's turn to speak and the moment we had all been waiting for. I was expecting all the passion and charisma that he brought to the confusingly non oscar nominated film 'When Saturday Comes'. I was disappointed. None of that charisma was present and as if he had forgot his lines he read for the most part straight off a script he had been given. So after a day that wouldn't have looked out of place in Peter Kay's Phoenix Nights, I realised protesting does work. Our day out in the middle of June partly resulted in Sheffield United receiving a compensation packet and in excess of twenty million pounds in the vaults of Sheffield United. A massive amount to go and spend on the world of footballs brightest sparks. What do we do? Buy Ched Evans for three million pound.

When applying to a university there are many essential things you have to look out for. You should consider the social benefits. For example, are there a lot of people, will there be societies and sports to keep you occupied and does it have a well thought of nightlife. You should then consider the academic benefits of the institution. Does it offer your course, where it is on the league table, how big is its library etc. This is where I differed from many. Sheffield Uni was my first choice of University probably from the age of eleven. This was before I knew I what I wanted to be or whether education even agreed with me. I wanted to go to Sheffield as it meant win or lose I could go and watch my team every week. Let's be honest most places do a History BA and if not Politics, Sociology or Psychology does a similar sort of job. Just as, you will always meet at least someone you get on with and surely there are even a couple of pubs you can keep yourself entertained in around Aberystwyth. This is where Sheffield University is unique for me, as it is the only place I can watch the team I support whilst being able to gain a degree. Ok there is Sheffield Hallam but Childhood Studies isn't really my cup of tea.

There are a few football related misconceptions I have made myself believe, that whilst living here I have found to be completely unfounded. The first of these is that Sheffield Wednesday fans do actually exist and that they are in fact numerous. Before I began living in Sheffield I had visions of a red and white utopia with Wendy fans being about as easy to find as a greasy spoon café on London Road. I now fundamentally know this is not true. I live all of five minutes away from Brammall Lane and I still see Blue and White shirts sporadically dotted around. When I go and play football at Goodwin I can't move for tripping over a pig (I can say that now as I live here). On my refereeing course that I partook in early on this year I was surrounded by them. It seemed every tutor we had and half those on the course was an Owl. God help Sheffield United in the future every referee there is will be of Blue and White persuasions. It's like Denmark, there's about three pigs for every normal person. This epidemic nearly influenced my sister when she was studying up here. She ended up playing for them. To her credit she wore the light of Red and White under her playing shirt to equalise the mortal sin she had partaken in. Let me say that is a good effort, as wearing two nylon shirts in April can get quite warm. To be honest it was a step up from her last team Millwall Lionesses, where as I recall a inter-club pre season friendly ended up with two players on crutches.

Another belief I had about Sheffield and Yorkshire in general was that everybody was about four times more pleasant than down South. For the most part it is true people from Sheffield are some of the warmest people you could wish to interact with. If you don't believe me just go to Greggs or Cooplands and you will understand what I mean. Men and women address each other with the word 'love' or 'duck' if that is not a happy place I don't know where is. However, this all changes when people walk through the turnstiles of Brammall Lane. There is something in the atmosphere of that place that converts these people into Red and White monsters. The woman who served you a Sausage Bean and Cheese Melt cannot help her self from shouting expletives against Kevin McCabe after a three nil defeat to QPR. The bloke that waited a whole minute and a half to get around you while your one geared bike crawled up a hill without as much as a beep, begins to proclaim physical action against Andy Taylor for his third misplaced pass in the succession of five minutes. This is multiplied by one hundred in the section I sit in or as we more affectionately call it 'God's Waiting Room'. I still to this day haven't heard anything positive to be said in this section of the ground.

So my final anecdote on my footballing life as a Blade growing up in London begins in the very London setting of Charing Cross overlooking a symbol of victory Trafalgar Square. It was 2008 this time and came after our third and final defeat in the play-off final to Burnley. We all slowly filtered in to the Chandos ready to adequately drown our sorrows and forget the events that had happened earlier. It was at that point that we received word from another one of our clan that he had been barred from the pub we were in. It had been over an altercation with wearing team colours within the pub as it might cause a problem with the three Burnley fans that were celebrating. After this was all sorted out or more likely ignored conversation quickly reverted to the standard shoulda, woulda, coulda dialogue of the last twenty years of United's history that usually follows a play-off defeat. It was in that moment I had a vision and could see how my life would pan out. Like a scene out of 'A Christmas Carol' I was taken to a pub that wasn't the Chandos (which had probably been converted into a Currys or a self storage store) but looked very much like it. On the outside of the pub I read a chalk board

'WATCH IT LIVE HERE: SHEFFIELD UNITED Vs ROCHDALE LEAGUE TWO PLAYOFF FINAL'.

As I got closer I had a look through the window and saw an older, more sizeable and balder version of myself making what could only be described as incoherent conversation to nobody in particular. Through the grunts and hisses I could make out certain names, 'Mergh....Graham Poll.....Mark Stein... Ergh.....David Unsworth....RARGH...CARLOS TEVEZ!'. In this moment I had not only seen that supporting Sheffield United may put me in literal bars as well as virtual ones. At this point I had the great realisation, that I was merely a cog in the footballing 'Circle of Life'.

The frustrations and anger of the generation that came before would be passed down to me the next generation and create an amplified version of the hardships and frustrations they had experienced. This cycle would carry on through generations after me and would eventually end with spontaneous combustion or alternatively one generation getting into Rugby or some other pointless sport like that.

Although I have put forward this prison metaphor, supporting Sheffield United for me has broadened my horizons. Whether walking into Parliament with a shirt that is inside out, singing in Annie's with a forty year old stag in Magaluf or freezing my five year old fingers off at a game at Kenilworth Road being a Cockney Blade has provided me with many experiences that those of my age and geographical location would have not had the chance to experience. So looking over my twenty-year affiliation with the boys from beautiful down town Brammall Lane I ask myself, If I had the chance to live my life again would I change anything. I always find myself coming up with the same conclusion. Of course I bloody would! Why couldn't I have been a Manchester United, Liverpool or Barcelona fan at least they have won a thing or two while I've been alive.

'Like Sheffield United,
Come fill me again,
Na..na.na.na.na.na....ohhhh!'

Selected Bibliography

Books

Balague, G (2005) *Rafa Benitez, Liverpool and the Path to European Glory*. London: Wiedenfield and Nicholson.

Dalglish, K (2010) *My Liverpool Home*. London: Hodder and Stoughton.

Davies, H. (1972) *The Glory Game: Year in the Life of Tottenham Hotspur*. Worthing: Littlehampton Book Services.

Kelly, S (1996) *Bill Shankly*. London: Virgin Books.

Higginson, S and Wailey, T (2006) *Edgy Cities*. Liverpool: Northern Lights.

Marx, K (1848) *The Communist Manifesto*. London: German Workers' Educational Society.

McCormack, P (2010) *Two Years in a Lifetime Following Bath City*. Derby: Peter McCormack – pmccormack@aol.com.

Miller, K (2003) *Stars in Stripes – The Official History of Bath City Football Club*. Bath: Bath City Football Club.

Magazines

Back Pass
Four Four Two
New Statesman
When Saturday Comes

Newspapers

Daily Mail
Liverpool Daily Post
The Football League Paper
The Guardian
The Non-League Paper

Websites

I Love Bath City – http://www.ilovebathcity.com
Spirit of Shankly – http://www.spiritofshankly.com

Films

Wailey, T. *Eight Days A Week/ Koln 2000*, (1998) Liverpool Artists Group

Music

Chi Lites, (1971) *Have you seen her*, Aklan, Chicago, Brunswick Records

Lightning Source UK Ltd.
Milton Keynes UK
UKOW031608231111

182584UK00005B/39/P